D. J. WEST

HOMOSEXUALITY

PENGUIN BOOKS

Penguin Books Ltd, Harmondsworth, Middlesex
AUSTRALIA: Penguin Books Pty Ltd, 762 Whitehorse Road,
Mitcham, Victoria

—

First published by Duckworth 1955
This revised edition published in Pelican Books 1960

Made and printed in Great Britain
by Hazell Watson & Viney Ltd
Aylesbury and Slough

31/3　　4/39p

PELICAN BOOKS

A477

HOMOSEXUALITY

D. J. WEST

CONTENTS

FOREWORD

No more appropriate moment could possibly have been found for the publication of a book on homosexuality than the present when, following a number of sensational trials and a considerable amount of public discussion, a Departmental Committee set up by the Government is studying the whole thorny problem. However, the success of Dr West's book will not be dependent upon such chance factors; it can stand on its own feet. His approach to the many and complex aspects of the subject is scientific and at the same time popular. Much harm has been done to it in the past by the extremists of various creeds, but the author is not one of them. Sceptical of any kind of rash generalization, he adheres to the doctrine of the multiplicity of the causes of homosexuality. Anxious to dispel any exaggerated beliefs in the unique strength of constitutional, hereditary, and endocrine influences, and naturally sympathetic to psychiatric and, in particular, psycho-analytic explanations, he nevertheless readily admits the significance of cultural and sociological factors. While averse to any attempt to force the almost limitless variety of individual characteristics among homosexuals into the artificial scheme of a typology, he does not dispute the prevalence of certain traits in individual members of the species and, even more, in groups of homosexuals. Where he favours one or the other of the traditional theories of causation, be it mother fixation and Oedipus complex or anything else, it is accepted only as a 'central theme' to be supplemented by a number of subsidiary themes.

In the field of treatment, too, prolonged psycho-analysis, though regarded as the most promising technique, is recommended only with reservations and for carefully selected cases. Reform of the penal law, which in the author's view should be the same for homosexuals and heterosexuals, is rightly placed very high on the list of priorities, especially for purposes of prevention; and 'treatment through imprisonment', in spite of the valuable work done in a few prisons, is labelled a contradiction in terms.

Some readers of the present book will recall to their minds the Conference on the same subject held at the Royal Society of Medicine in London in April 1947, when the urgent need for a 'fact-finding commission' was stressed and some of the principal problems to be investigated were outlined by various speakers. There was no inclination at that representative meeting to minimize the exceptional difficulties of doing worthwhile research in this field – difficulties some of which are also indicated by Dr West, and which explains why the recommendations of the Conference have so far not been carried out. Whether the present Departmental Committee will be able to fulfil the functions of such a fact-finding body we do not know. Meanwhile, although no single author's book can be a full substitute for the multi-disciplinary approach of a team of experts as envisaged in 1947, a book such as the present one satisfies a real need in preparing the soil.

HERMANN MANNHEIM

London, March 1955

INTRODUCTION

NOT so long ago, sexual topics were avoided in polite conversation and young persons were carefully shielded from too early awareness of what was considered the more unpleasant side of life. Ideas have changed, and works on hitherto taboo subjects, such as marital adjustment and birth control, now circulate freely. But although lip service is paid to the ideal of an open attitude to sex, prudery and obscurantism linger on, especially in relation to homosexuality, on which topic many persons still preserve an attitude of old-fashioned, superstitious abhorrence. In recent years, however, the subject has come more into the open. Some sensational trials involving prominent men, and the subsequent appointment of the Wolfenden Committee to inquire into English law on homosexuality, have caused extensive debates in Press and Parliament. Although at times the discussions have shown more of the heat of controversy than the light of understanding, at least they have broken the long conspiracy of silence and brought this serious social problem out of the atmosphere of school-room smut and into the arena of public debate. More and more people want to know the facts of the matter, and this book sets out to give the general reader a sober account of the information available, as well as to consider the implications calmly in the light of common sense and modern knowledge.

It is now realized that homosexuality is an extremely common condition and that the only reason why psychiatrists and law courts are not completely swamped with cases is that the great majority of those affected neither seek psychological advice nor fall into the hands of the police. Apart from the specialized writings of psycho-analysts, medical literature devotes but scant consideration to homosexuality, and even this is not always well informed or free from bias. The subject is only just beginning to receive the serious scientific attention that its importance warrants. Yet homosexuals are so numerous that nearly everyone, whether he realizes it or not, has one or more among his acquaintances. But it is not just on account of the number of such persons that the matter is of general concern. Occasional homosexual feelings may be experienced by anyone, and those responsible for training children, administering the law, or advising on public morals cannot fulfil their duty to the community if they keep themselves in ignorance of certain facts. Homosexuality is a part of life that intelligent people should know about and understand. Unhealthy ignorance causes an almost unbelievable amount of misery and frustration.

In view of the cloak of secrecy with which our society shields itself from the spectacle of sexual abnormality, and the uncompromising denunciation by moralists of what they call 'unnatural vice', it is no surprise that the average person looks on homosexuality with rooted aversion, and that his ideas about it are crude. Male homosexuals have been variously regarded as degenerate personalities, moral pariahs who obstinately persist in tasting forbidden fruits, effete, 'pansy' types incapable of natural manliness, dangerous seducers of the young, victims of circumstance, sufferers from psychological disorder, cases of glandular disease, or even the forerunners of a new biological type – the third sex. None of these views completely fits the known facts. After perusing the account which follows the reader will form his own conclusion, but it may be useful to know from the outset the author's own outlook. It seems to him that children are not born with the sex instinct specifically directed to one sex or the other. Exclusive preference for the opposite sex is an acquired trait, and involves the repression of a certain amount of homosexual feeling which is natural to the human being. Some adults fail to become completely inhibited in this respect, and though they have normal, happy relations with the opposite sex, they can still enjoy occasional homosexual activities as well. One may perhaps disapprove of their behaviour, but they are not necessarily psychologically ill. On the other hand, the completely homosexual man, one who is repelled rather than attracted by feminine charms, really suffers from an abnormal inhibition, the origin of which can often be traced to psychological causes early in life. In such a case, the flight from heterosexual relations is a neurotic symptom, produced in much the same way as other irrational fears and inhibitions. Freud put the same basic idea more elegantly when he wrote: 'Freedom to range equally over male and female objects – as it is found in childhood, in primitive states of society, and early periods of history, is the original basis from which, as a result of restriction in one direction or another, both the normal and the inverted types develop.' [1]

1. Freud, S. *Three Essays on the Theory of Sexuality* (translated J. Strachey). London, 1949, p. 23, footnote.

This book deals primarily with male homosexuality, because in men the condition causes more obvious social problems and has been studied more intensively by psychiatrists. Homosexuality in women is sometimes called lesbianism, the name deriving from Lesbos, an island in the Aegean, where the Greek poetess Sappho lived in the fifth century B.C. She gathered about her a circle of female admirers and wrote passionate verses in praise of lovely maidens. Lesbians have usually been less vocal and obtrusive than male homosexuals, so less has been written about them, and they have not been legislated against nor so fully investigated.

As with ordinary attraction between men and women (heterosexuality), homosexual feelings are a mixture of varying proportions of animal passion and sentimental fondness. Since normal copulation between persons of the same sex is impossible, homosexuals depend for reaching climax (orgasm) on methods of mutual stimulation that normal couples would regard as mere incidental indulgences leading up to intercourse. Kissing, fondling, close bodily contact, and mutual masturbation are the chief forms of homosexual love-making. There are also the possibilities of intercourse via the mouth (*fellatio*) or the bowel (anal intercourse or sodomy). But these methods of sexual gratification are by no means confined to homosexuals, and not all homosexuals indulge in them. The distinguishing feature of homosexuals is not that in love-making they prefer any particular type of bodily stimulation, but that they prefer their own to the opposite sex.

The thought of intimate contacts with their own sex disgusts many normal persons, but some homosexuals are even more appalled by the idea of relations with the opposite sex. The typical homosexual man, even if he has no positive revulsion against women, is completely uninterested in them. They fail either to excite him sexually or to arouse his emotions. Such exclusive homosexuals are sometimes called inverts, but it is best to avoid the term because it has become associated with the unproven theory that complete inverts are a race apart, different in their genetic make-up from the rest of humanity. The name bisexual is applied to persons who experience varying degrees of attraction to both sexes, but this also is an unfortunate term because it implies a separate category [159]. In reality one finds every conceivable gradation between absolute heterosexuality and complete inversion. In this book the term 'inversion' is avoided, the unqualified word 'homosexual' signifies 'more or less exclusively homosexual', and the adjectives 'partial' or 'occasional' are inserted when necessary.

D. J. W.

Part 1

THE BASIC FACTS

1

Homosexuality in Various Communities

I. PRIMITIVE PEOPLES

To most people today homosexual indulgence seems so
obviously abnormal that it may come as a surprise to learn
that many communities do not share their attitude. In a
recent survey of anthropological literature the investigators
Ford and Beach found that in 49 out of 76 (that is 64 per
cent) of the primitive societies about which information was
available some form of homosexual activity was considered
normal and acceptable. In some societies male homosexuality was universal [58]. They quote several examples of this.
For instance the Siwans, a small North African tribe, who
live by raising crops and domestic animals, expect all men
and boys to engage in homosexual sodomy, and think a man
peculiar if he does not have both male and female affairs.
Among the Keraki of New Guinea the young men are introduced to anal intercourse at puberty by older men, and
thereafter spend the rest of their bachelorhood doing the
same to other initiates. They have to pass through these two
stages of first passive and later active homosexual sodomy
before they can achieve full social status and have relations
with women [18]. The Kiwai have similar customs; they
believe sodomy helpful in making young men strong [119].
The Aranda of Australia carry the custom a stage further.
Their youths commonly go through a stage of homosexual
'marriage' in which they live as a 'wife' with an older
bachelor for several years until the elder partner breaks
away and takes a female wife.

Some communities have a recognized class of men, variously called *berdaches*, *alyhas*, or *shamans*, who are intermediate in social status between men and women. They
dress like women, perform women's tasks, and even marry

men. Sexually they take the passive role in sodomy. Special
ceremonies have to be gone through before a man is recognized as a proper *berdache*. In some tribes the *berdaches*
carry their pretence to femininity so far that they imitate
female functions, scratching themselves to simulate mens-
trual blood or stuffing their clothes with rags to simulate
pregnancy.

George Devereux made a study of the homosexual system
among the Mohave Indians, a warrior race who inhabited
the South-West of North America. Youths who did not fit in
with the usual pursuits of the male members of the tribe
went through an elaborate ceremony which changed their
sex status. Henceforth they were *alyhas*, who lived and
dressed as women and were permitted to set up house with
a 'husband'. The *alyha* usually made an industrious wife,
and had a quite respectable position in the community. The
alyha's husband, however, had to suffer a certain amount of
teasing, especially when his 'wife' insisted that he observe
obsolete taboos in honour of an entirely imaginary pregnancy. In this community there was also a recognized class
of exclusively homosexual women [44]. In general, however,
the occurrence of extensive lesbianism has rarely been noted
by anthropologists.

The Big Nambas, a cannibal race of the New Hebrides,
were also noted for their institutionalized homosexuality [90]
as were the Zuni Indians of North America [17]. Ruth
Benedict was particularly impressed by the fact that the
berdaches had a definite position in the social structure and
were able to lead useful lives. Often they excelled and took
the lead in women's occupations, but some of their husbands
were weaklings who preferred a self-supporting *berdache* to
an economically dependent wife. Ruth Benedict inclined to
conclude that the sense of guilt and inadequacy and the
social failure of many homosexuals today is a secondary
consequence of the strain of social disapproval and not the
result of the condition itself. Like the Zuni, the Siberian
Chukchee also had a class of men-women who enjoyed great
prestige. They were called *shamans*, and were credited with

supernatural powers. They lived as 'wives', taking the passive role in sodomy. Their 'husbands' were allowed to have female mistresses as well, and sometimes the *shamans* too had mistresses and fathered children of their own [58].

Some tribes have an attitude of indifference to homosexual practices, considering them matters of no importance. The Manus of New Guinea for instance, preserved a very rigid moral discipline with regard to heterosexual relations, which they surrounded with a host of taboos and inhibitions, but homosexual acts they viewed with laughing unconcern [140].

In some tribes, though homosexual practices take place between adult males, sodomy is avoided. Others will not tolerate homosexual practices in any shape or form. Malinowski says of the Trobriand Islanders that, although they permit affectionate intimacy and embraces between male friends, perverse acts are effectively kept down by contempt, ridicule, and scoffing. Exposed culprits may kill themselves. The Trobrianders' language includes phrases descriptive of sodomy, but individuals always insist that such acts are a thing of the past. The homosexual practices common among the natives confined in gaols, mission stations, and plantation barracks Malinowski attributes to the forcible segregation of men used to regular sex activities [133]. There are other tribes, even stricter than the Trobrianders, who put to death any men found committing sodomy. The general rule seems to be that in any community in which homosexuality is said to be rare there are strong pressures brought to bear against its open manifestation.

In primitive communities, therefore, one finds every shade of attitude from complete indifference, through amused tolerance and institutional recognition, to severe condemnation.

2. HISTORICAL TIMES

Homosexuality is as old as humanity and occurs as much in advanced civilizations as it does in primitive cultures. In the 'Terminal Essay' to his translation of *The Arabian Nights*,

Sir Richard Burton instances with monotonous pertinacity one example after another of homosexual practices past and present. He claims that such practices have always been endemic over a vast area of the globe, including the countries bordering the Mediterranean and a great part of the East, especially India, China, Japan, and the Pacific islands. His rambling discourse covers such diverse matters as male brothels both ancient and modern, scandals in French society under the Second Empire, lewd treatment of prisoners in Egypt during the Napoleonic wars, male prostitutes on the caravan trails of the Middle East, the uninhibited behaviour of South Sea Islanders, romantic male love in classical Greece, and the debauches of the Caesars. After wading through all this it is hard to resist the conclusion that homosexual behaviour constitutes a fundamental human tendency that may crop up at any time [28]. Sometimes it is found linked with the religious beliefs and ceremonials. Burton states that 'in Rome as in Egypt the temples of Isis were centres of sodomy', and similar practices took place among 'grand priestly castes from Mesopotamia to Mexico and Peru.' (Vol. x, p.227).

References to the matter in the Old Testament writings indicate that among the ancient tribes of Israel homosexuality was both practised and condemned. In Genesis xix occurs the story of a group of debauched men of Sodom who stormed the house where Lot was, demanding: 'Where are the men which came in to thee this night? Bring them out to us that we may know them.' Lot offers his virgin daughters instead. The same story with slight modifications also appears in Judges xix. In this case a female concubine was proffered in place of the man they sought. The Rev. Sherwin Bailey [9] contests the meaning of some words in the old biblical texts. He doubts whether the sins that caused the destruction of Sodom had any connexion with homosexual vice.

For a perfect example of a homosexually orientated civilization none can compare with classical Greece. When Plato wrote so sublimely of the emotions and aspirations of love he was describing what we should call perversion. Male homosexual sentiment permeated the whole fabric of Greek society. Homosexuality meant more to the Greeks than a safety valve for excess of lust; it was in their eyes the highest and noblest of passions. They idealized the love of man for man as much as present-day Western civilization idealizes romantic love between men and women [124].

The subservient role played by Greek women probably helped foster this curious attitude. Greek civilization was essentially a man's world. Their literature dealt almost entirely with male pursuits and the masculine point of view. Courage and nobility of mind, indeed all the most admired virtues, seemed essentially manly attributes. The women lacked education and lived in seclusion in their own rooms. There was no domestic life as we know it, so that men of culture looked always to their own sex for stimulating companionship [182]. On matters of sex the Greeks had an uninhibited outlook. They held sensual enjoyment an important part of life and were not afraid to express their sentiments. The human body, and especially the body of the athletic young male, was admired as an object of great beauty, a fitting subject for eulogistic poems and exquisite sculpture. The influence of this ideal on the art of the period is well known.

It seemed natural to the Greeks that men should be passionately attracted by beautiful youths, and it was usual for an older man to take under his wing some favourite youth and to act as his special friend and mentor. The Doric states observed this custom especially strictly. A man failed in his duty if he did not become the guardian of one younger than himself whom he could instruct in the manly virtues, and a youth felt disgraced if he failed to win such a friendship [23].

Homosexual sentiment abounds in ancient Greek legends, and was prominent in the heyday of Greek civilization as well as during its decay. Writers pictured homosexual love as a lofty passion that raised men above themselves. In his *Symposium* Plato wrote:

And if there were only some way of contriving that a state or army should be made up of lovers and their loves, they would be the very best governors of their own city, abstaining from all dishonour, and emulating one another in honour, and when fighting at each other's side, although a mere handful, they would overcome the world. For what lover would not choose rather to be seen by all mankind than by his beloved, either when abandoning his post or throwing away his arms? He would be ready to die a thousand deaths rather than endure this. Or who would desert his beloved or fail him in the hour of danger? The veriest coward would become an inspired hero, equal to the bravest, at such a time; Love would inspire him.

(Jowett translation.)

The Spartan and Theban armies were organized on just this theory, regularly making sacrifices to Eros before battle. The celebrated Theban Band, long supposed invincible, consisted of pairs of lovers fighting side by side. When finally they were annihilated at the battle of Chaeronea, even their conqueror wept at the sight of the three hundred lying dead together [45].

The Greeks did not encourage indiscriminate infatuations. Socrates' fascination for youths brought him no credit. Moreover, the cult of effeminacy in young men and the buying or selling of sexual favours evoked the strongest disapproval. The penal code of ancient Athens included various provisions against homosexual abuses, some of which dated from Solon's enactments in the sixth century B.C. Though relations between adult citizens were permitted, Solon forbade a slave to have association with a free-born youth on pain of a public whipping. Though others might do as they thought fit, later legislation provided for the removal of all civil rights from any Athenian citizen who prostituted his body for money. The legal code also took special care to protect children from seduction. For an outrage against a minor a man could be sentenced to death or to a heavy fine. A father (or guardian) who prostituted his son for gain was liable to severe punishment, as was the man who took advantage of the boy, although the boy himself, provided he was under age, suffered no legal penalty [142].

Even among the Greek States attitudes differed. In Elis and Boeotia homosexual indulgence was perfectly respectable, whereas in Ionia, close to the Persian border, it was attributed to foreign influence and condemned. In Athens and Sparta homosexuality achieved respectability by virtue of the ideal spirit dominating such friendships, but indulgence for its own sake was considered sordid. Plato, in *The Laws*, Book I, takes a strong line against those who seek to satisfy their lust without regard to time, place, and circumstance. Socrates seems to have been somewhat less strict. In Xenophon's *Memorabilia* (I, iii, 8–11) Socrates makes light of the fact that someone has been caught flirting with a handsome youth, remarking that he might well try the same thing himself. Again, in Xenophon's *Banquet* (iv, 23–30) Socrates is playfully accused of having been responsible for young Critobulus forming an unseemly violent passion for another young man. Socrates defends himself by saying that the passion in question dated from the young man's school days, and claiming to have had a moderating influence on Critobulus. He goes on to discourse on the need for moderation in love and the danger of having one's head turned by kissing a handsome youth, but his friends tease him for not following his own precepts. One gains the impression that, whatever may have happened in actuality, the Greek ideal of homosexual love was a chaste attachment, one that expressed itself more in fine sentiments and generous deeds than in sexual activity or passionate jealousies.

Nothing could be in greater contrast to the outlook in some ancient Roman literature. Gone are the spiritual aspirations, the moral scruples, the niceties of argument. Homosexuality is depicted as a luxurious vice, to be practised together with rape, sadistic torture, and every form of revolting orgy. The *Satyricon* of Petronius portrays a thoroughly degenerate society in which everyone is bent on the pleasure of the moment. The tale opens with the attempted seduction of a young man by a much older one, but the

young man learns nothing from his unpleasant adventure
and at once tries forcibly to seduce a still younger person.
Suetonius's *Lives of the Caesars* is a sorry tale of debauchery.
Nero's disgusting and cruel orgies, in which men and women
suffered equally, reached the depths of squalor. He had
Sporus, his favourite, castrated, after which he went through
all the ceremonies of marriage and made the unfortunate
youth his 'wife'. Apparently many emperors were tarred
with the same brush, even Julius Caesar whom one senator,
the older Curio, called 'every woman's man and every man's
woman'. True or not, the taunt reflects the morals of an age
in which such behaviour was commonplace.

Study of the sexual habits of Greece and Rome serves to
confirm what has already been deduced from anthropological studies, namely that homosexual instincts soon make
themselves apparent whenever they are given a free rein.
The consequences can be good or bad according to how the
community handles the situation. In Greece homosexual
love was made to serve the highest ideals of the time. For
the later Romans, homosexual lust merely added variety to
their debaucheries. Not since the decline of classical Greece
has male homosexuality been raised to the status of a
desirable ideal, though pale reflections of ancient Sparta have
from time to time appeared in various militaristic systems.
At the time of the Crusades, the cult of masculine valour,
the hero-worship, the great emphasis on manly fortitude and
valour, the tradition of the pure woman to be admired from
afar, doubtless helped to foster homosexual tendencies. The
homosexual behaviour attributed to such bands as the
Templars must be understood in the light of this background. A somewhat similar situation prevailed in recent
times in Nazi Germany when the Hitler Youth banded
together for the sake of a mystic, manly ideal that over-rode
all family ties [147].

Leaving the ancient world and coming nearer home, the
history of our own civilization shows that the cultivation of a
severely repressive attitude has consistently failed to eradicate the homosexual problem. In each century one finds the

question of homosexuality arising. Even in periods when detection meant death the practice was known to be widespread. The popular notion that this is a social problem of the present day, due to a recent relaxation of moral standards, can be disproved by the briefest excursion into history [184].

Elizabethan literature has homosexual allusions. Shakespeare himself wrote sonnets apparently addressed to a youth. According to Montgomery Hyde, that other great dramatist Christopher Marlowe only escaped execution for homosexual offences through being murdered in the nick of time in a public house brawl. In 1631, for acts of sodomy, the Earl of Castlehaven and two of his servants were dispatched on the scaffold and the gallows respectively [98]. In the eighteenth century convictions and executions were frequent, but the male brothels and homosexual clubs thrived in London [99]. A renowned meeting place, the White Swan, headquarters of the Vere Street Coterie, was exposed in 1810, and seven men were sent to the pillory in the Haymarket. A huge mob gathered and behaved with unusual brutality. Street vendors hawked missiles, which the angry crowd hurled at the prisoners, causing severe injuries.

A curious little eighteenth-century book entitled *Plain Reasons for the Growth of Sodomy in England* (Anon., c. 1730) [6] shows that even in those days homosexuality was considered a social problem. The author attributes the prevalence of the vice to the molly-coddling of boys and the cultivation of effeminate habits by young men. He deplores the custom of sending young boys to kindergartens run by women. He thinks the young men's habits of foppish attire, continental manners, indolence, and tea-drinking breed milksops. The influence of the Italian opera he considers particularly pernicious, for it is well known (he alleges) that sodomy is thought a trivial matter in Italy, so that no sooner does a stranger set foot in Rome than the procurers rush to ask if he wants a woman or a young man.

The nineteenth century was full of scandals, from the suicide of the Foreign Minister Castlereagh because of the

fear (probably delusory) of being denounced, to the imprisonment of the playwright Oscar Wilde after three sensational trials [102]. Wilde was convicted largely on the
evidence of self-confessed male prostitutes and blackmailers
who turned Queen's Evidence and thus went free. A similar
affair in our own time (1953) was the second trial of a young
peer, who was convicted and sent to prison on the evidence
of two airmen who, though they fully admitted homosexual
offences, were prepared to give evidence for the Crown. They
received immunity from prosecution.

In the period between these two famous trials public
opinion in Britain has changed. When Wilde was sentenced,
it is said, prostitutes in the street outside the Old Bailey
lifted their skirts to dance in glee, and sermons on the
subject were delivered throughout the country. The learned
judge expressed his utmost indignation at the evidence of
corruption of the most hideous kind and regretted that the
maximum penalty he was allowed to give was totally inadequate. But even in 1895 there were some more sober
counsels. The famous editor W. T. Stead wrote: 'Should
everyone found guilty of Oscar Wilde's crime be imprisoned,
there would be a very surprising emigration from Eton,
Harrow, Rugby, and Winchester to the gaols of Pentonville
and Holloway.'

3. ANIMAL BEHAVIOUR

Homosexual behaviour occurs commonly enough in animals
as well as man, especially in the mammalian species. The
sight of dogs mounting each other and making copulatory
movements is a familiar street spectacle, and countrymen
know how often cows and cockerels do the same. Scientists
have reported the same observations more systematically [13,
58]. It appears that female mammals frequently display masculine coital behaviour towards receptive members of their
own sex, and sometimes males imitate the behaviour of receptive females, so that other males become excited and
mount them. Such happenings are more frequent when
animals of the same sex are segregated together, but also

occur in natural surroundings. Seemingly the more sexually excitable animals are the ones most prone to homosexual activity.

These animal reactions may not have the same causal basis as similar behaviour in human beings. In most cases, homosexual responsiveness is commoner in the young; as the animals mature they learn greater discrimination in their choice of sex partner. Some animals will only mount another of the same sex when no opposite-sexed partner can be found. However, among primates, which are the animals closest to man in the evolutionary scale, unmistakable homosexual alliances have been observed between mature adults even when members of the opposite sex were available [203]. But there is one notable difference between human and animal behaviour in this respect. Many human homosexuals react only to their own sex and find themselves completely inhibited by persons of opposite sex. Animals, though they may retain their bisexual potentialities, and respond readily to either sex, do not normally develop an exclusive preference for the same sex.

The closest parallel to human homosexuality has been induced experimentally in male adult rats by prolonged segregation from females. The longer the males were kept apart from females, the more homosexual activity manifested. Some males, when given access to females after long separation, evinced little interest in them and continued for an indefinite period to prefer their own kind [104].

In another interesting experiment with rats, Rasmussen [162] showed that homosexual behaviour could be increased by giving male animals an electric shock whenever they attempted copulation with females.

Dr F. A. Beach, a great expert on animal sexuality, considers bisexual responsiveness a part of our mammalian instinctive heritage. He has this to say about human homosexuality: 'In our society sexual contact between members of the same sex is considered extremely undesirable. Various social goals and ethical laws are violated by the homosexual individual, but to describe his behaviour as "unnatural" is to depart from strict accuracy' [14]. The scattered references to deviant sexual practices found in the literature of almost every age lend ample support to this view. Homosexual behaviour seems to arise from some deep-rooted natural urge which finds different expression in different cultures. One must, however, guard against the facile assumption of many homosexual apologists that what is biologically natural is necessarily desirable or permissible. Murder does not become any more tolerable because it can be viewed as the expression of a natural impulse. A policy of tolerance towards sexual deviants should stem from other considerations.

2

The Incidence of Homosexuality Today

OFTEN it is easier to study the ways of primitive tribes and historic civilizations than to examine contemporary culture, for only by dint of great mental effort can a man stand back and view dispassionately his own cherished beliefs and customs. In attempting to estimate the frequency of homosexuality in the community today, one must guard against the tendency to minimize what is unpleasant or inconvenient. Estimates by normal folk, based on their personal observation, are always too low. They do not care to suspect their own acquaintances, and the deviants themselves are at pains to disguise their peculiarity from family and friends. A well-known psychiatric authority, in the preface to the second edition of his book on sexual perversions, remarked that he had been astonished by the number of acquaintances and colleagues who had consulted him since the appearance of the first edition, although they had shown no outward sign of abnormality [1]. When addressing a meeting of a medical society recently, another psychiatrist who had written on the subject of homosexuality remarked that he had been deluged with pathetic requests from persons seeking treatment. On a different plane, but equally indicative of the homosexual problem seething beneath the surface in present-day society, is the quantity of correspondence from would-be sympathizers received by prominent men whose names have been publicized in trials on homosexual charges.

Police statistics prove that male homosexuality is common, but can give no indication of its true extent, since the majority of illegal sex acts naturally take place secretly behind closed doors. *The Times* for 13 May 1954 drew attention to the rapid increase in the frequency of prosecutions for homosexuality. In the period 1900 to 1909 there was an

annual average of 13 such prosecutions per million males
over the age of ten. In the period 1920 to 1924, the corresponding figure was 32; in the period 1950 to 1952 the figure
had increased to 107. Table II in the Wolfenden Report
[198] shows a steady rise in the number of prosecutions for
indictable homosexual offences in England and Wales, from
390 in 1931 to 2,504 in 1955. That prosecutions are now more
numerous does not mean homosexuality has increased. A
more vigilant police policy could easily account for the
change. One consequence of frequent prosecutions is that
the already overcrowded British prisons, in addition to cop-
ing with their regular criminal inmates, have to house between one and two thousand men serving sentences for
homosexuality.

Men who are themselves homosexual, and experienced in
making contacts, are relatively well placed for judging the
proportion of their fellows similarly inclined. Their estimates vary. Some promiscuous homosexuals assert that most
men will indulge on occasion. This is probably an exaggera-
tion, due to the homosexual's understandable desire not to
be considered a type apart. It may be true that some experienced homosexuals rarely find themselves rejected, but
if so the likely explanation is that they learn to recognize and
concentrate their attention exclusively upon men likely to
respond. However, the anonymous author of a conscientious
little book entitled *The Invert*, reports, after some sober consideration, that up to five per cent of men are predominantly
homosexual [5].

The assertion that about one in twenty of all adult males
are predominantly homosexual seems at first almost incred-
ible, but there is good evidence to show that the figure cannot be far from the truth. Whenever a substantial group of
men live in close relationship, whether at college, in the
army, or elsewhere, a few among them will be recognizable
to all but the most innocent as obvious homosexuals, and
these obvious or blatant types will in turn know of other men
in the group no less homosexual than themselves who have
kept their inclinations secret from their normal fellows. In

fact any person who is at all sophisticated in these matters knows that the few thousand cases dealt with annually by the police represent no more than a tiny minority of scapegoats.

For practical purposes the psychiatrist and the sociologist need not know the exact proportion of practising homosexuals in the community so long as they understand the virtually limitless extent of the problem. But the more scientifically minded have long wanted to have an exact figure. The earliest estimates made by such investigators as Havelock Ellis were little more than shrewd guesses based on common-sense considerations plus the testimony of confessing homosexuals. Ellis himself believed that two to five per cent of Englishmen were predominantly homosexual [51].

The Germans attacked the matter more systematically [98]. Dr Magnus Hirschfeld circulated a questionnaire to 3,000 German male technology students and 5,721 metal workers. According to the replies 2·3 per cent of them were exclusive homosexuals and 3·4 per cent were partial homosexuals. Since only a half of those who were sent forms returned an answer, the result cannot be reliable. Hirschfeld sought to obtain confirmation by questioning homosexual men who, by virtue of their experiences, would know the extent of the homosexual activity among their own business and social groups. By this means he arrived again at approximately the same figures [97].

In more recent years further estimates have been made. In 1929 G. V. Hamilton published a survey of the lives of 100 married men and 100 married women. Seventeen of the 100 men reported having had some homosexual experience after the age of 18 [88]. In 1947 an American psychologist reported the results of a questionnaire study submitted to a class of adult students in advanced psychology. He prepared the students for the questionnaire by a course of preliminary instruction and assured them of the secrecy of their replies. By this means he secured answers from 111 members of the total class of 138. Of those who replied 27 per cent admitted at least one adult homosexual episode leading to orgasm [54].

In 1948 all previous work on these lines was put in the shade by the publication of a monumental survey on the sexual behaviour of American men prepared by the zoologist Dr A. C. Kinsey and his collaborators [112]. These investigators collected a sample of over 4,000 American men, representing as far as possible a cross section of the white community. They gave all the men confidential interviews in which they questioned them exhaustively about their sexual habits. They estimated that in the United States about 4 per cent of the white males are exclusively homosexual all their lives, and that over a third of all males admitted at least some adult homosexual experience. Their criterion of homosexual practices was contact with another man leading to orgasm. They introduced a seven-point rating scale of homosexuality, giving a maximum of six points to those who had orgasms only with other men, a minimum of 0 points to men who had orgasms only with women, and a mid score of three to men who had orgasms equally with either sex. They found that there were more men with the intermediate scores than with the maximum of 6, so that partial homosexuals were even commoner than complete inverts. They found, for example, that nearly a quarter of all men indulged in some homosexual activity, and that 10 per cent were more or less exclusively homosexual in their outlets, for a period of at least three years consecutively.

In considering these findings one must keep in mind that Kinsey concerned himself with bodily indulgence rather than the investigation of subjective feelings. The evidence of societies in which homosexual practices are universal, and the frequency of homosexual incidents in prison camps and other places where men are confined together without women, shows that most normal men are potentially capable of enjoying homosexual experiences. Kinsey has shown that a very high proportion of normal men do in fact indulge occasionally even when women are available. But the man who only occasionally, and perhaps only in special circumstances, indulges in homosexual excitements, and then returns happily to his wife, is less of a social or psychiatric problem than the man who is incapable of ever enjoying a woman. Kinsey's percentages are swollen by the large number of uninhibited and highly-sexed men who will satisfy themselves with either a male or female partner. The real psychological problem, however, is the hard core of complete homosexuals, represented by Kinsey's 4 per cent, who eschew women all their lives.

One important outcome of the Kinsey exploration was the conclusion that homosexuality is not an all-or-none condition, and that it is not always permanent and unalterable. Many men who were predominantly homosexual in their teens and early twenties married later and settled down to normal sex relations. On the other hand as high a proportion as 10 per cent of the younger married men admitted having concurrent homosexual experience, and there were also some who changed from exclusively heterosexual habits to exclusively homosexual ones. Another interesting point was the evidence from older men. Their testimony gave no indication of any substantial change in the incidence of homosexuality from one generation to the next.

Kinsey's work met with a storm of criticism, much of it abusive and ill-informed. The viewpoint of the majority of critics was succinctly expressed by the naïve comment of the doctor who wrote, in the *Practitioner*, vol. 172, 1954, p. 357: 'These unseemly explorations during growth are better unrecorded; one would certainly get just as high percentages from the obliquities of other appetites, of gluttonies and pilferings. It would have been a cleaner world if Kinsey had stuck to his rats.'

In fact no one has been able seriously to dispute Kinsey's findings with regard to the prevalence of homosexuality. He and his collaborators were alive to the need for caution. They remark in their report:

We ourselves were totally unprepared to find such incidence data when this research was originally undertaken. Over a period of years we were repeatedly assailed with doubts as to whether we were getting a fair cross section of the total population or whether a selection of cases was biasing the results. It has been our experience, however, that each new group into which we have gone has provided substantially the same data. Whether the histories were taken in large cities, in small towns, or in rural areas, whether they came from one college or from another, a church school or a state university or some private institution, whether they came from one part of the country or from another, the incidence data on the homosexual have been more or less the same [112].

Kinsey and his colleagues checked their figures in a variety of ways. They were acutely aware of the dangers of lies, exaggerations, and suppressions, and took great pains to guard against them. The interviewers were experienced and specially trained, and of course familiar with the slang terms and mode of life associated with different sexual patterns. A deliberate cheat would have soon put himself under suspicion by inconsistent responses to the many interrelated questions fired at him in the course of the interview. 'Retakes' of case histories, in which the same persons were questioned again after a lapse of years, and also comparison of the results of different interviewers, confirmed the substantial accuracy of the data collected, particularly with regard to the incidence of homosexual activity. The investigators tackled the possibility of unfair selection by approaching whole groups, such as college classes and fraternities, or all the occupants of particular lodging houses. Bias due to the omission of persons unwilling to cooperate was eliminated when everyone in a group was prevailed upon to give the required information. The figures for these complete groups, as well as those for almost complete groups, were much the same as the figures for the total sample.

They applied other checks. They compared the incidence of homosexuality in different places, in different religious and social groups, and at different age levels, all of which showed that their over-all percentages were reasonably representative and consistent. When possible they checked their findings against some independent criterion. The statements of married couples were compared one with the other, and the testimony of men and women on the incidence of activities involving both sexes was compared. Recollection on such points as the age when pubertal changes took place were compared with the results of direct observation. The checks all served to confirm the essential soundness of their estimates. In fact their investigation was about as painstaking and as scientific as such a project could be. The figures in the report may not be 100 per cent accurate, but at least they give a better picture of the true state of affairs than any previous research. Some slight inaccuracy either way would be of little practical significance. A knowledge of the exact percentage of homosexuals in various grades of society is of academic interest, but a realization that they abound everywhere is a conclusion of interest to all.

The popular press in England gave the Kinsey investigation a shoddy reception. Some newspapers hypocritically condemned the publication as pornographic or morally subversive and at the same time printed sensational excerpts under lavish headlines. In Doncaster magistrates went so far as to order confiscation of copies of Kinsey's second book, but later decided against declaring it obscene.

For a reasonable appraisal of Kinsey's work one must consult psychological literature [115, 72]. One recurrent criticism is that Kinsey limited himself to a study of actual behaviour, refraining from any deep examination of emotional attitudes or attempts at psychological discussion [19]. This was deliberate, for Kinsey wanted to keep his research strictly objective and leave the theorizing to others. But psychiatrists in particular have been irked by the absence of any meaningful interpretations of the behaviour reported by Kinsey. A too rigid adherence to the 'objective' behaviouristic approach can be misleading, for in matters of human sexuality what a person feels is often more important than what he does. Quantitative observation tells only a part of the story. Judged solely on the criterion of the number of orgasms per week, a man may appear to have a full and satisfactory sexual life when, in reality, he is being driven to over-indulgence on account of inner fears and compulsions. In the case of homosexual behaviour, Kinsey did not distinguish clearly between casual homosexual adventures, such as might be thought a part of normal development, and the compulsive seeking out of fresh contacts by the confirmed sexual deviant. Kinsey might have found out a lot more if he had taken into account the underlying motives behind sex behaviour, but his discoveries are none the less important for lacking completeness. His donkey work has given a firm factual basis for further research, and one only hopes psychologists and psychiatrists will make the most of it.

Publication in 1953 of the second Kinsey report [113], this time on the sexual behaviour of American women, brought to light a wealth of information on the extent of female homosexual practices. Of course previous investigators had dealt with the same question, but never before had anyone conducted such a large-scale inquiry. In 1929 Katharine Davis had published a survey of the sex habits of 2,200 American women, 1,200 of them college graduates [41]. She found that more than a sixth of the women had had overt homosexual experiences. The frequency was higher in the case of college graduates and single women. There were as many again who had had intense emotional relationships with other women, but without actual bodily indulgence. In a later American study, published in 1940, in which a group of 153 women were questioned, less than four per cent admitted actual sexual practices with other women, but as many as 21 per cent reported having had more intense mental or physical attachments to women than to men friends [118].

The Kinsey research went into greater detail and showed that active lesbianism, although widespread, is less common than overt male homosexuality. The fact that convention allows kissing and other manifestations of affection between women might give a false impression. In his sample of American men Kinsey found that by the time they reached the age of 45 at least 37 per cent had had some homosexual contact leading to orgasm in the course of their adult life, although of course in many cases it was a rare or isolated experience. In contrast, the corresponding figure for his sample of nearly 6,000 white women was only 13 per cent. He also found that many of the women who reported homosexual experiences had had them during only a short period of their lives. Relatively few women remained predominantly homosexual for many years and nearly all of those who did were unmarried women. In his sample about 4 per cent of the single women remained more or less exclusively homosexual in their outlets throughout the period from 20 to 35 years of age. The corresponding figure for single men was about three times as great. The permanent, complete homosexual was thus decidedly less common among women.

A substantial proportion of male homosexuals have sexual experiences with many different people, but Kinsey found that lesbians more often restrict themselves to one or two partners. It seems to be a general rule among both homosexuals and heterosexuals that men are more promiscuous than women. One reason for this may be that men are more easily tempted into unfaithfulness because they are more easily aroused sexually by psychological stimuli, such as the sight of a good-looking person or the recollection of past pleasures. It is quite normal for young men to be aroused to the point of erection several times a day without having any actual physical contact. Women, on the average, are less readily excited by casual suggestions or associations in the absence of bodily stimulation. The partner's physical appearance is not of such paramount importance to women, and they can go without sex for longer periods than men because they are not being so frequently aroused.

Kinsey's views as to the relative infrequency of promiscuity among lesbians conform to the impressions of most observers and are confirmed by Hans Giese's recently published five-year study of 2,000 homosexual men and 100 homosexual women. According to him, female homosexual relationships are usually lasting and firm, whereas the males are usual inconstant and unstable [75]. Most homosexually inclined women are affectionate and faithful; they indulge plentifully in caresses, but stop short of full physical expression [196]. One professional woman, herself a homosexual, in a contribution to the *American Journal of Psychiatry*, points out that only a small minority of lesbians belong to the promiscuous, commercially minded group who frequent night clubs. According to her, lesbians suffer just as male homosexuals do from feelings of loneliness and being misunderstood by their fellows. They fear their own degrading impulses, and some of them seek relief in alcohol [130]. The difference in the sexual habits of female as opposed to male homosexuals helps to keep lesbianism less publicly conspicuous and accounts for the relatively small number of lesbian prostitutes.

After these Kinsey studies the enormity of the social problem of homosexuality can no longer be denied. No one knows the true incidences of the different grades of homosexuality in England. The Wolfenden Report states frankly that no inquiries comparable to Kinsey's have been made in England, and that the majority of the medical witnesses who gave evidence to the Committee admitted that they really didn't know what figures would be likely to be found. The only systematic inquiry they could quote was that of a psychologist who investigated 100 British male undergraduates and found that 30 per cent had had homosexual trends and fantasies, and that 5 per cent retained them at the age of twenty plus. With their traditional system of sex segregation at schools and at the older universities the English have earned the reputation abroad for a particularly high incidence of 'vice anglaise'; but assuming the incidence in Britain to be really no greater than in the United States, that would mean that there are nearly a million predominantly homosexual men in the country. Sensible discussion has long been hindered by a concentration of public attention on the small and untypical minority caught by the police. A little reflection will show how futile are the hopes of eradicating homosexuality by psycho-analysis or imprisonment unless the entire 'normal' population is prepared to act as doctors or jailers to the 'perverts'.

The ubiquity of homosexual tendencies in the animal

world, as well as in many human races, and the fact that homosexual practices continue unabated in our own civilization in spite of strong condemnation, all goes to suggest that such behaviour is just one manifestation of the uncurbed biological sex drive. In fact there is much to be said for the view that learning and experience rather than any innate quality of the biological sex urge are the causes of the normal preference for a mate of the opposite sex. Given the right circumstances – living among the Siwans for example – anyone might practise homosexuality. In our civilization most individuals repress all such tendencies in themselves and regard any who indulge in them as 'perverse' or 'unnatural'.

The analogy of incest shows how a human society can repress fundamental sex urges. Animals will mate with others of the same brood, but almost all human societies have an intense horror of sexual contacts between members of the same family. Some primitive societies have excessively elaborate kinship taboos and marriage regulations. The incest taboos of our own society, though less obtrusive, are sufficient to cause very strong repression of sexual feelings relating to brothers and sisters and parents. In most persons the repression is so complete that, not only is incest unthinkable, but it is hard for them even to imagine their parents having sexual relations, and sexual topics are much more easily discussed with strangers than with members of the family. This widespread repression shows that mankind has long striven to obliterate incestuous feelings which, though they may be biologically natural, threaten the very existence of a civilization based on family units.

Many adults genuinely believe that they have never had the slightest incestuous or homosexual feeling, but this may mean no more than that they have repressed all such thoughts at an early age. Of course the taboo against homosexuality is less strong than that against incest, possibly because, when viewed dispassionately, homosexual indulgence seems relatively harmless.

3

Homosexual Types

WHAT sort of people are homosexuals? The word conjures up a particular type – the effete, precious-mannered young man with mincing gait and feminine tone of voice. In practice the majority of homosexuals possess no such obvious signs. The affectedly effeminate group is a minority which attracts undue public attention and gives rise to a stereotyped idea of the male homosexual that is about as unfair as the stereotype of the beak-nosed, money-grabbing Jew. Those who imagine that they can invariably pick out 'one of them' at a glance are certainly mistaken. Homosexuals are to be found anywhere and everywhere, in all types of occupation and in every social class, but as most of them possess no obvious distinguishing features, either of appearance or manner, the unsophisticated remain in ignorance of their existence.

Male homosexuality has long been associated in the public mind with Bohemian artistic and theatrical circles. Before ever Oscar Wilde suffered his legal exposure, his band of 'precious' young men provoked unfavourable comment. The Gilbert and Sullivan comic opera *Patience*, first performed in 1891, contained the famous song about the 'particularly pure young man'. Other groups also have a reputation for homosexuality, for instance sailors and boxers, who are the reverse of effete or theatrical, which only goes to confirm that there is no special character common to all homosexuals. Moralists have proclaimed that homosexuals are degenerate types, and prison officials, such as Sir Norwood East, have pointed out the high incidence of homosexuality among criminals and persons of weak mentality [177, 48]. In contrast, as homosexual literature never tires of pointing out, the greatest writers and musicians include a goodly proportion of known homosexuals. The realistic viewpoint accepts homosexuality as a universal potentiality that may develop in response to a wide variety of factors. Neurotic fears of sex, disappointment in love, an all-male background, guilt about women, all these things may contribute and tip the scales towards a homosexual development. Thus the mere fact that a man is homosexually inclined tells us nothing about his character. He may have developed that way as a result of too many scruples about women, or he may have cultivated homosexuality because it affords easy sexual gratification without trouble or responsibility. The possession of homosexual inclinations no more defines a man's character than the possession of a nervous twitch.

Acceptance of the fact that homosexuality affects a substantial proportion of the population means the abandonment of some common notions about homosexual 'types'. The popular idea that all male homosexuals have effeminate body build, girlish outlook and mannerisms, or a weak character, is a complete misconception. Among the homosexual multitude all types of physique and character may be found. Misconceptions about physique readily arise on account of a minority of male homosexuals who affect peculiar mannerisms amounting to a crude caricature of femininity, including simpering attitude, swaying gait, over-smooth movements, and lisping voice. The motives behind this odd behaviour, which may be so habitual as to become automatic and unconscious, vary from a real desire to play a woman's role to a need to advertise for a mate. When such mannerisms become extreme, the man-in-the-street recognizes them and gets the impression that all male homosexuals must be half women.

Psychiatrists holding the view that the cause of homosexuality must lie in some inborn biological quirk have looked so hard for traces of femininity that sometimes they have found them. A wide variety of physical traits have been allegedly associated with homosexuality, including small stature, excess fat, wide hips, smooth skin, a feminine distri-

bution of pubic hair, narrow shoulders, a boyish face, luxuri-
ant hair, an inability to whistle, and a 'too good-looking'
appearance. That some of these traits are contradictory is
sufficient ground for caution. In all probability feminine
traits occur as often among normal men as among homosexuals, but homosexuals who happen to be effeminate are
readily spotted and remembered.

Systematic studies of samples of known homosexuals have
failed to demonstrate any consistent deviations from the
average measurements of comparable groups of normal men
[199]. Weil, examining a group of 380 mature male German
homosexuals, concluded that they had a significantly greater
height, longer legs, and wider hips than a normal group.
However, another investigator, Wortis, criticized his findings
and claimed that the results were vitiated by the fact that
the normal and homosexual groups came from different
districts with different average heights [200]. Comparing
Weil's homosexual measurements with published data from
other groups of German males showed no significant difference in height or hip and shoulder width.

In another series of measurements, published by two
American psychiatrists, the ratio of shoulder width to pelvis
width was further from the feminine average in a group of
homosexuals than in a corresponding group of normal men
[95]. All such investigations have to be viewed with scepti-
cism because of the great difficulty of securing an unselected
group of male homosexuals.

In one American study of 342 psychotic male patients, 37
of whom were known to be repeatedly and persistently indulging in homosexual practices, no significant peculiarities
in height, weight, torso length, or hip-shoulder measurements could be discovered among the homosexual group.
An apparent difference in pubic hair distribution impressed
the investigators, a proportion of the homosexuals having
genital hair tending towards the female type with a hori-
zontal upper margin. But the figures were too small to be
statistically significant. One can but agree with Barahal's
conclusion: 'Experience has shown that body measurements

are so variable, even in the so-called normal group, that ... it is impossible to reach any conclusion from such measurements. The same applies to other traits and characteristics frequently attributed to homosexuals, such as those pertaining to hair distribution, mannerisms, pitch of voice, and so forth' [10].

2. PSYCHOLOGICAL CHARACTERISTICS

Generalizations about homosexual temperament are no safer than generalizations about homosexual physique. Clinical psychologists have tried to develop tests to distinguish homosexuals from normals. Some of these are really tests of neurotic tendency, working on the supposition that anxious or inhibited responses to words or pictures with sexual connotations indicate conflicts about sex and probable homosexuality. As will be explained later (Chapter VIII), the supposed connexion between homosexual and neurotic tendencies is much disputed. Other tests depend on the assumption that male homosexuals will react more like women than like normal men. To give a very simple example, in the 'Draw-a-Person' test, the majority of men and women choose to draw first a figure of their own sex. If a man draws a woman first this has been held to suggest homosexual tendencies. Grygier, in a most competent survey of the tests so far developed, concludes that none is reliable [85]. What is accepted as typically masculine or feminine in tastes and attitudes varies with age, social class, and educational background, and furthermore many men with inverted sexual preferences still preserve masculine tastes in most other respects. When the American investigators Terman and Miles first introduced a psychological test for masculine and feminine mental traits they applied it to male homosexuals with odd results [185]. Their test was a 456-item questionnaire, including word associations, statement of moral attitudes, interests, opinions, character preferences, and so on. The average man and woman gave radically different scores on the test. It is now generally admitted that this is due at least as much to individual training factors as to innate differences between the sexes. Be this as it may, it is interesting that male musicians and artists gave score averages that were almost female, whereas women athletes, doctors, and scientists gave scores that were almost male.

The test was given to 77 men described as passive homosexuals and to 46 said to be active homosexuals. The first group produced scores more typical of females than males, whereas the second group scored more 'masculine' than the average soldier. The authors were inclined to conclude that there were two qualitatively different types of male homosexuality. In my view a more likely cause for the differences was the way the two groups were selected. For the passives they first contacted a subject in gaol, and he brought his friends, who in turn brought their friends. Most of them were prostitutes. The second group was recruited from the U.S. Disciplinary Barracks at Alcatraz. It is not surprising that the aggressive criminal group were more masculine than the average, or that the prostitutes, whose chief advertisement is an imitation of femininity, should give female scores. The results merely show that there is as wide a range of temperaments among homosexuals as in the population at large.

Slater devised a male-female vocabulary test which he believed to be more discriminating than the lengthier Terman and Miles test. It depended upon the principle that certain words were more familiar to men than to women and vice versa. The average score of 37 male homosexuals who were given the test deviated in the expected direction, that is towards femininity, but there were wide variations of score and the homosexuals were clearly a mixed group [173].

It is a fallacy that all male homosexuals have effeminate characters and all lesbians are 'masculine', but it does seem to be the case that certain homosexuals show a temperamental bias towards features normally associated with the opposite sex. This fact has been used as an argument in favour of the existence of a group of persons – the 'true inverts' – who supposedly possess a constitutional tendency to contrary sexual habits and disposition [83]. But the argument loses its force in the face of modern anthropological research which shows that many of the temperamental characteristics popularly defined as 'masculine' or 'feminine' are the result of cultural training and are not biological sexual distinctions. Margaret Mead, in particular, has called attention to wide differences in the traditions of masculinity and femininity. Among the Tchambuli, for example, there is a sharp division between male and female roles, but in contrast to our own culture it is the Tchambuli women who do the productive work, dominate in social organization, and take the initiative in sexual relations. The men have a more decorative function. Supported by female labour, they spent their time on art and in the production of ceremonial dances. The ideal Tchambuli woman is efficient, businesslike, loyal, and comradely; but for the Tchambuli man it is normal to indulge in affected manners, catty gossip, and jealous squabbles.

Among the Mungudumors, another primitive people studied by Margaret Mead, both men and women were far more aggressive than is normal for the most masculine in our culture. Their society had no place for tolerance and affectionate relationships, and their men were in a perpetual state of jealous hostility, fighting and insulting each other in a ceaseless battle to possess the best women. The male ideal was a life in splendid isolation within a stockade housing many wives to look after him and only a few puny male relations who would not challenge his supremacy. The wives were only a degree less hostile, quarrelling among themselves and refusing to help each other's children. Both men and women liked brief, passionate sexual contacts in which foreplay consisted of biting, scratching, ripping clothes, and tearing ornaments [138].

From observations of this kind Mead contends that dominance or submissiveness in social behaviour are not sex-linked characteristics, and that therefore any society that defines masculinity and femininity in such terms will inevitably have a large number of temperamental misfits.

Some theorists label all such misfits 'latent homosexuals', but this is wrong. Temperamental non-conformity does not necessarily imply deviant sexual impulses, although the difficulties that these misfits encounter in their attempts to establish normal relations may cause some of them to seek refuge in homosexuality [139].

Some psychiatrists believe, and there is evidence to support their view, that male homosexuals fall into two contrasting categories known respectively as *active* and *passive*. The active type is forceful and masculine in his love-making, while the passive is gentle, yielding, coy, and liking to be chased. If sodomy occurs, it is the active partner who penetrates the passive. The active type tends to display his masculinity, to cultivate athletic pursuits, and to reject all feminine traits. The passive type is more likely to adopt pseudo-feminine mannerisms. The use in homosexual circles of such slang expressions as 'bull' and 'butch' or 'cow' and 'queen' shows that some at least must conform to type.

According to some theorists different causes operate to produce these two types. The passive type, often regarded as the 'true' invert, is thought more likely to possess feminine physique or to have some glandular disturbance, whereas the active type is merely looking for a substitute for a woman. But the evidence on these points is flimsy. The homosexual man with predominantly passive sex habits does not necessarily affect feminine manners or possess feminine physique. Wortis quotes two cases of passive homosexuals with markedly effeminate mannerisms who had undoubtedly masculine physique [200], and I have known two men (the history of one is given later) habitually passive in their sexual relations who were effeminate neither in body nor in manner. A great many homosexuals, possibly the majority, prefer mutually reciprocated sex activity where neither partner dominates. Many adopt the active or passive roles as occasion demands. Some begin by taking only the active role in sodomy, thinking that by so doing they avoid being really 'queer', and end up by taking the passive role in order to please more youthful partners.

Nevertheless, a minority of homosexuals identify themselves very definitely with the female sex and try to imitate women in everything. They have a passion for cosmetics, dress, and housewifery. They may go to fabulous lengths in their endeavours to play the female role, even entreating surgeons to remove their genitals. Such individuals generally prefer to take the passive role in sexual relations simply because they regard it as more feminine. Brown has suggested reserving the term invert for persons having this strong cross-sex identification, which may well have separate causes from homosexuality in general [27], since some of the men who delight in female pursuits or obtain pleasure from dressing up in women's clothes are nevertheless thoroughly heterosexual.

Although there is no such thing as a characteristic homosexual type, either of physique or temperament, nevertheless certain traits appear with particular frequency among homosexuals. Some of these traits doubtless arise from the same psychological factors as have initially been responsible for turning the individual away from normal outlets; others may be the direct consequence of the difficult, secretive life a homosexual has to lead [186]. The most important trait, certainly the one most noticeable to a psychiatrist, is the pronounced sense of guilt and shame. It manifests in various ways. Some homosexuals accept all too readily the popular sentiment of condemnation and go through life in an agony of self-torture over their immoral desires. They strive after continence, but sooner or later yield to temptation, and then they pay for it in untold pangs of remorse and disgust. The sense of guilt may become so acute that the unfortunate individual can fit in nowhere and do nothing right because his terrific feeling of inferiority virtually paralyses all initiative and destroys all pleasure in human contacts. An actual case of this kind is described in Chapter 5.

Psycho-analysts usually attribute this feeling of guilt to a carry-over from early neurotic conflict. The same guilty fears that prevent the young person developing normal sexual interests, causing him to turn instead to homosexuality, are later responsible for the adult's acute guilt feelings. On the other hand, it is arguable that the attitude of abhorrence that society reserves for sexual deviants provides adequate reason for their sense of guilt. Doubtless both factors contribute.

Many homosexuals succeed in time in conquering up to a point their initial sense of shame. Sometimes consultation with a doctor who will accept them as they are gives them a new feeling of assurance. Mixing with other homosexuals who take their condition as a matter of course eases their conscience and also removes their feeling of isolation. They gain the security of a group membership, and discover a milieu in which they can express themselves freely without fear of persecution. This sense of belonging to a group, even though a persecuted minority, gives considerable relief to the guilt-ridden homosexual. A short time ago in England homosexuals could imagine themselves the worst freaks or sinners on earth simply because they had no knowledge of the many thousands of others similarly affected. As it is, the continual parade of homosexual scandals in the popular press, accompanied as they are by the usual sanctimonious expressions of horror, does nothing to alleviate the distress of the many young persons fighting a lonely battle with unconfessed sexual conflicts.

With increasing experience of life, and accumulated contacts with other homosexuals, guilt feelings recede, but signs of underlying insecurity often remain. Many suffer throughout their lives from an abnormal sensitiveness, a quickness to feel slighted, a suspicion that they are not properly accepted by their colleagues. Some develop a protective brazen front, an 'I'm as good as the next one' attitude. Such over-compensation for inner insecurity has a lot to do with the aggressively brazen behaviour of those groups already mentioned who affect outrageous manners. Evelyn Hooker has suggested [101] that some of the traits and attitudes said to be typical of the warped personality of some homosexuals are in fact characteristics regularly found among all rejected minority groups: they are really 'traits of victimization', that is defensive responses to a hostile world. For example, the obsessive concern of homosexuals with their problem recalls the obsessive concern of Jews and negroes with race and colour. Special attitudes, such as 'protective clowning' and 'hatred of himself and his own group' as well as 'attitudes of dependence and passivity' are all commonly found both in homosexual and in other minority groups. Homosexuals are also liable to depression. In a study of 200 neurotic soldiers, half of them with known homosexual tendencies, Karl Lambert [117] found a history of attempted suicide or severe depression much more common among the homosexuals. O'Connor, reporting on a small series of suicides and attempted suicides, found a homosexual problem in a half of the cases [151].

Apart from their characteristic sense of guilt, homosexuals vary so much that it is virtually impossible to pick out any one feature common to all. Writers on the subject, even medical writers who should know better, carelessly throw out generalizations without an atom of validity. One reads that homosexuals are depraved, or exhibitionists, or (and this usually from the homosexuals themselves) that they are more 'alive' and 'sympathetic' than the humdrum mass of humanity. In reality some homosexuals suffer from neurotic fears and anxieties, and some are self-assured and hard as nails; some are vain and ostentatious and some are shy and quiet; some are cowardly and some are heroes; some are effeminate and some are brutes. Since all these types are represented, psychologists can all too easily pick out examples to suit their own pet theories. Those who choose to believe the condition is a sign of moral degeneracy, on a par with drug addiction, alcoholism, and criminal tendencies, can find plenty of examples among the prison and criminal population of men who readily satisfy any and every sexual whim without the slightest pang of conscience. On the other hand, those who believe that the over-attachment of the young boy to his mother causes homosexuality can equally well pick out examples, especially among only children, of shy, pampered men who have never broken away from an adoring mother. Those who believe that homosexuality springs from narcissism – that is to say, love of self to a pathological degree coupled with inability to form a give-and-take relationship with other people – can readily point out vain, attention-seeking individuals who are prepared to put on a show of simpering mannerisms for the benefit of any male willing to dally with them. The question of causation will be dealt with later. Suffice for the moment to say that there is probably some truth in all these divergent views. Seemingly anyone can develop homosexuality given the right conditions, but the causes will differ from one case to the next. A mentally defective criminal and a musical genius may both be homosexual, but their characters and the influences that have moulded them will be radically different.

3. HOMOSEXUAL SOCIETY AND LITERATURE

Although few generalizations can be made about individuals, cliques of homosexuals possess very definite characteristics. This is partly because individuals of a particular type are specially attracted to such cliques, and partly because homosexuals, like any other unwanted minority, react by forming their own special outlook and conventions in defiance of the hostile majority. One of the consequences of the presence in our midst of large numbers of men living under the threat of ostracism and prosecution is the existence, unknown to most normal persons, of a vast underworld of sexual deviants. In normal company the homosexual preserves a front, pretends to feelings he does not have, and keeps his real interests and inclinations to himself: but among the secret community of his fellows he can throw off the mask. In this strange underworld they have their own little social coteries, their own conventions and slang, their own favourite bars, restaurants, and meeting places. When one place develops such a reputation that it is raided by the police they simply move on to another. Entry into this camaraderie is a matter of visiting the right places in the right clothes and knowing the right conversational gambits and *doubles entendres*. A newcomer puts on just the shadow of a meaning look, remarks with just a tinge of the accepted inflexion, 'Isn't it *gay* in here?' and, if he is a presentable young man, he is lonely no more. An uninformed bystander would notice nothing untoward. Among these circles the initiated make themselves understood by the use of a slang that is almost a Masonic code. Homosexuals are 'gay' or 'queer', one markedly effeminate is 'camp', one out for money is 'rent', one who is too noticeable is 'screaming'. To be looking for sex is to be out for 'trade', to be dressed in women's clothes is to be 'in drag'. All this and much more Rodney Garland describes in his very frank novel, *The Heart in Exile* [71].

Homosexuals as a group are very conscious of being a persecuted minority. Several countries have magazines for homosexuals that conduct a perennial campaign for greater tolerance. The monthly entitled *One*, published in Los Angeles, circulates among American homosexuals and rather pathetically addresses itself to clergymen and others begging for sympathetic understanding and deploring the condemnation of homosexuals by organized religion. Among continental magazines for homosexuals are the Scandinavian monthly *Vennen* (The Friend), an international monthly *Der Kreis* (The Circle) published since 1936 in Zurich and containing articles in French, German, and English, *Arcadie*, published in Paris, and a Dutch monthly *Vriendschap*. Some of them include numerous photographs of attractive young men as well as personal advertisements for companions. In addition, the International Committee for Sexual Equality publishes, in Amsterdam, a bi-monthly *Newsletter* giving information about Church pronouncements, changes in police procedure or in the law, and similar matters of interest to homosexuals. Invariably they give long reviews of all new novels that touch upon homosexual topics. A fair number of these have appeared in recent years, some of them by well-known authors.

The apologetics produced by these homosexual magazines are sometimes most amusing. In their propaganda for social tolerance they lose no opportunity to claim common ground with great literary and historical personages whose deviant sexual habits have become publicly known. Doubtless the intention is to link homosexuality with socially valuable qualities, but the reasoning is often as muddled as that of the anti-vice campaigner who wants to prove that all homosexuals are evil persons. Names like Plato, Leonardo, Michelangelo, Tchaikovsky, Walt Whitman recur again and again in the homosexual magazines, but the discovery that all these great men were sexual deviants is worth about as much as a discovery that they all had fair hair. Homosexuality is so common in all walks of life that one would expect any group of persons whose intimate lives have been recorded to contain a quota of homosexuals. The Kings of England, for example, whose renown is based on accident of birth rather than specially good or specially bad characteristics, include several whose homosexual tendencies were well known. William Rufus's behaviour was so scandalous that he was refused a sanctified burial by the Church. Edward II kept the notorious Piers Gaveston and other favourites. James I's favourite, Robert Carr, is said to have escaped punishment for murder because he threatened to make public his relations with the King, and William III is said to have been in love with Albemarle. Those interested in historical by-ways may perhaps identify other homosexual monarchs, but the exercise merely shows that kings share the common passions of humanity.

Writers are specially prone to expose their private emotions to public scrutiny, and the world of literature provides a number of examples of famous homosexuals. Verlaine boasted that he was one of:

> The chosen ones, the servants of the good Church,
> Of which Plato would be Pope and Socrates the nuncio.

André Gide made no secret of his male loves [74]. In one of his works, *Corydon,* he creates a fictitious doctor who expounds at great length a scientific justification for homosexual practices. Marcel Proust, author of the analytic masterpiece, *A la recherche du temps perdu,* infused life into his love passages by drawing upon his own passionate experiences as a homosexual lover. He had a liaison with one Albert Le Cuziat, keeper of a male brothel, to which he even contributed some of his family furniture [137].

In a few cases the love of woman for woman forms the basis of a literary creation, as in the late Miss Radclyffe Hall's rather pathetic novel *The Well of Loneliness.* Although the book has since been reissued, when it first appeared in 1928 the publishers, Jonathan Cape, withdrew it from circulation at the request of the Home Secretary. A few months later a Bow Street magistrate condemned the book as obscene and ordered the destruction of all copies. The decision was upheld in spite of an appeal.

The poetess Renée Vivien, who wrote in the first decade of this century, deserves to be called the modern Sappho. Her verses sang the praises of lesbian love, and she even went so far as to build herself a Greek villa in order the better to cultivate the atmosphere of her classical predecessor.

Within the underworld homosexual society, various classes and groups can be distinguished. In big cities there are always a few notorious bars or clubs patronized by the exhibitionistic set who like to flaunt themselves in public. They dress in the latest fancy fashions, and cultivate loud, pseudo-feminine mannerisms. Some of them make such use of powder and perfume as to be hardly distinguishable from the dolled-up prostitutes whose livelihood depends upon parading themselves. But homosexual cliques are not all like this. Some low-class bars, where the patrons include small-fry blackmailers and men wanting to sell their bodies, present an outward appearance little different from any other rough haunt, except for the presence of a sprinkling of middle-class gentlemen. At the other end of the scale, the fashionable smart sets which meet in clubs and private parties enjoy an air of snobbish sophistication. Other groups meet socially in each others' houses as do ordinary cliques of friends, except that the class composition is more mixed, as homosexuality tends to cut across the usual social barriers. In these circles, conversational virtuosity, a frothy wit, and an ability to gossip knowledgeably about the theatre are assets second only to the possession of a trim figure and pretty face. But their relationships are brittle and fickle, and beneath the protective social gloss many are frustrated and unhappy. Membership of these groups tends to remove the homosexual still further from ordinary society. Many men come to feel that they can only 'be themselves' on these occasions, with the result that they lose interest in ordinary pursuits and feel bored in normal company. Frequent contact with these groups, and with their ceaseless sexual gossip, tends to foster promiscuity and attitudes of unhealthy cynicism.

These comments apply only to homosexual society as it manifests in large centres of population where unorthodox groups can find a footing. Many homosexuals, probably the majority of them, have no contact with such groups, and live in isolated and unobtrusive fashion. They may not even know about homosexual cliques, or they may refrain from mingling because they fear the risks of exposure or because they disapprove of homosexual affectations. In many cases their sense of shame makes them the last persons to enjoy exhibitionistic behaviour.

For the minority who find attraction in homosexual cliques, the 'gay life', as they like to call it, has a certain fascination. The sense of self-importance derived from belonging to an 'underworld' group, and the enjoyment of laughing behind society's back, compensates them for inferiority in other directions. They can feel a little superior to normal men living dull, routine lives. By mixing in these circles and cultivating promiscuous habits some ordinary young men find they can make contacts beyond the scope of their usual humdrum environment. Having no wives or children to tie them, they can travel easily, and wherever they go they can be sure of making contacts among what has been called the 'homintern'. But sooner or later the dreariness of cultivated artificiality makes itself felt, and the thrill of hunt and conquest gives place to the insecurity of a life of brief encounters. The histories of some homosexuals suggests the enactment of a preordained tragedy, a sort of rake's progress. In youth they hardly recognize themselves as different from the rest. Later they think they must be passing through a temporary phase. Then they have to admit, after fighting against the idea a long time, that they have a real homosexual fixation. As they get acquainted with others like themselves they come to accept their inverted sex feelings as a matter of course. Gradually they get more and more taken up with homosexual groups, adopting the current slang and attitudes, until eventually, except for formal relationships, at work, they have little real contact with the normal world. Life becomes a series of short-lived 'affairs'. Eventually the ageing homosexual finds himself on the shelf, lonely, without home or family, left pathetically and compulsively hanging about lavatories or trailing his old haunts trying to bribe himself into the company of young men. The normal man, restricted as he may be by the routine of family life, has no cause for envy.

While homosexual coteries and homosexual literature provide compensation of sorts, and afford some shield against the sharp jabs of contempt from the rest of the society, many fail to achieve a satisfactory, lasting adjustment. Some, of course, conquer their difficulties, or even put them to good use in callings that demand tolerance and understanding of other people. Some settle down with a partner of like mind, sharing each other's lives like any married couple, but it has frequently been commented upon how often such arrangements come to grief [75]. After years of promiscuity many male homosexuals find it hard to overcome the urge to hunt out someone fresh, and a long-standing partnership may be quickly jettisoned in favour of some fresh fancy. Unlike a marriage, which involves legal and economic obligations and the responsibility of children, the homosexual partnership has no protection from swift dissolution. Nevertheless, in spite of the absence of stabilizing factors, and in spite of the necessity for concealment, a surprising number do succeed in maintaining mature relationships which long outlast the disappearance of sexual passion.

Peter Wildeblood [195] has vividly portrayed the problems of the homosexual 'way of life', as indeed have a host of novelists and playwrights. An important systematic survey has recently been completed by Gordon Westwood for the British Social Biology Council. He questioned a large sample of volunteers from the homosexual population at large, exploring their backgrounds, attitudes, habits, choice of jobs, and so on. His report[1] will provide a reliable source of information about the realities of the situation, and will undoubtedly confirm that homosexuals are merely a collection of ordinary human beings, neither specially gifted nor specially evil, who react in different ways to their common problem.

1. G. Westwood. *Minority*. London (Longmans Green), 1960.

4

The Legal and Social Problem

I. INTIMIDATION AND BLACKMAIL

AFTER all the public discussion on the matter in recent years, no thinking person can any longer maintain that homosexuality concerns just an insignificant minority of freaks. But a formidable task confronts any investigator into the social implications of homosexuality. Anglo-Saxon society brands the male homosexual as criminal or worse, with the result that thousands upon thousands of seemingly respectable citizens lead a Jekyll-and-Hyde existence, part of the time posing as normal and part of the time moving in the homosexual underworld. One consequence of this state of affairs is a high incidence of intimidation and black-mail. Fear-ridden homosexuals, especially those in prominent positions, make easy game for blackmailers. In a lecture published in 1954, the Rt Hon. Earl Jowitt, Lord Chancellor of England from 1945 to 1952, made the surprising declaration that when he became Attorney-General in 1929 he was impressed with the fact that 'A very large percentage of blackmail cases – nearly 90 per cent of them – were cases in which the person blackmailed had been guilty of homosexual practices with an adult person' [106]. The Wolfenden Report states that of 71 cases of blackmail reported to the police in the years 1950–3, 32 were connected with homosexual activities. Contrary to popular belief, the homosexual who denounces a blackmailer does not enjoy immunity from prosecution. The Wolfenden Report quotes the case of a man and his sexual partner, who was blackmailing him, both receiving nine months' imprisonment for a first offence as a result of the victim appealing to the police.

Apart from the menace of professional blackmailers the

homosexual also runs the risk that any one of the friends
he has trusted may, in a moment of jealousy, anger, or indis-
cretion, give him away to relatives, to his employer, or to
the police. In recent years the United States authorities have
become acutely aware of the risk of blackmail in relation to
men serving abroad [84]. Foreign service has an attraction
for the homosexual who has no family ties and likes to
travel and meet new people all the time. The danger lies in
the possibility of an amorous encounter with some stranger
who may be in contact with a foreign power. An enemy
agent might force information out of a homosexual by prey-
ing upon his fear of exposure.

Although homosexuals tend to congregate in London, the
frequency of prosecution per head of population is less there
than in the country at large. The Wolfenden Report records
that 480 adult men were convicted of homosexual offences
committed in private with consenting adult partners in
England and Wales during the three years ending March
1956. In the Metropolitan Police District over the same
period there were only 10 such conviction, 5 of which arose
from complaints made to the police and 5 as a result of
inquiries into other matters, such as larceny and blackmail.
In the same three-year period there were only 9 such convictions in the whole of Scotland. The Report on Sexual
Offences by the Cambridge Department of Criminal Science
brings out the same point [158]. In 1954, the frequency of
prosecutions in the London Metropolitan Police District
(7·4 per 100,000 of population) was only a half what it was
in the other areas of England and Wales investigated. Of
the smaller cities, urban areas, and county areas the last
named showed the greatest frequency of prosecutions for
homosexual offences 16.9 per 100,000. Convictions for offences
between adults in private are mostly the result of incrimi-
nating statements made to the police by former contacts who
have been caught. In 449 cases, that is 94 per cent, of the 480
convictions mentioned in the Wolfenden Report, the men
charged made statements admitting their guilt. Some do so
in the hope of 'getting it over quickly' and avoiding pub-

licity. Some more hardened types escape the penalty by refusing to make any statement.

The punishments awarded vary erratically. The Wolfenden Report analyses 155 convictions for buggery between
consenting adults. 31 were bound over or discharged, absolutely or conditionally. 31 were put on probation. 75 were
given up to 2 years' imprisonment, and 10 got 2 to 5 years.
A curious legal anomaly, which makes for a still more erratic
distribution of punishment, is the existence of Local
Authority By Laws against nuisance and indecency in public places, in particular, parks and public lavatories. These
bye laws provide for penalties by fine up to five pounds. The
Wolfenden Report points out that for the same type of behaviour one man may receive only a small fine under a by
law while another might get two years in prison for gross
indecency.

Peculiar sex laws lead to peculiar abuses. Young thugs
specialize in enticing older men to make illicit advances so
that they can browbeat and rob them, secure in the knowledge that their victims dare not seek police protection. A
suspect homosexual can be pronounced guilty on circum-
stantial evidence that would be quite insufficient to convict
a robber. Some magistrates are so disturbed by sexual aberrations that their approach to homosexuals is conspicuously
harsher than their approach to the ordinary criminal. In
1953 a Member of Parliament resigned his seat after being
convicted; his offence consisted of looking at young men in
bars and public lavatories. He was found guilty on the evidence of two policemen who trailed him, one of whom,
under cross-examination, was forced to admit to making
false statements. Whatever the rights and wrongs of a particular case, it is easy to see how an innocent man might be
trapped. The present law puts too much responsibility on
the police and is almost an incitement to corruption.[1] The
account published by Peter Wildeblood of his own experiences of arrest and trial drew attention to the dangers of
injustice in such cases [194]. Convicted homosexuals fre-

1. For a case in point, see *News of the World*, 24 April 1955.

quently complain that in Court the case against them was exaggerated or over-stated in order to secure conviction.

In the United States the branch of the police force known as vice squads has met with much criticism, and responsible lawyers have questioned the justifiability of their methods of so-called 'entrapment'. One policeman acts as decoy or 'bait' and approaches the suspected sex offender. If the suspect commits himself at all, the policeman's partner moves in and together they make an arrest. The man acting as decoy may pose as a fellow homosexual and even go so far as to make sexual advances in order to make sure the suspect gives himself away. The regular defence for such unsavoury tactics is that 'rats must be trapped'. However, no argument can get round the plain fact that the duty of any police force is to prevent breaches of the law and not to provoke them for the sake of making an arrest. Corruption in some American vice squads seemingly does not stop short at provoking offences. In his article 'Vice Squad', in the magazine *Collier's* for 28 May 1954, Albert Deutsch describes how policemen have made fortunes by accepting bribes and protection money and by blackmailing sexual offenders. But not all the men who extort money from homosexuals are genuine policemen. Deutsch quotes the case of a vice squad impersonator who was tried in New York City for blackmailing a wealthy student to the tune of some 20,000 dollars. With the help of confederates this man had lured his victim into a compromising situation, brought out a bogus police badge, and told the terrified student that he was to be arrested on a charge of homosexuality. Of course the student paid up, but the demands got too big, and ultimately he went to the authorities. The supposed vice squad man turned out to be a well-known crook who specialized in blackmailing homosexuals.

In the introduction to his book, *Sex Variants*, the psychiatrist G. W. Henry tells of the personal tragedies that often follow from vice squad activities [93]. One of the techniques of the vice squad is to 'persuade' arrested men to give away the names of all the friends they know who are homosexual.

Dr Henry describes the case of a socially prominent man who returned to his home in an American town after an absence. Unaware that a vice crusade, accompanied by much newspaper publicity, was in full swing, he readily accepted an invitation to call at the police station. When he got there the police told him that they had a sworn statement from a man who said he had had sexual relations with him. After the police had assured him that anything he said would be strictly confidential, he naïvely admitted having had occasional homosexual experiences when away from his wife. He was at once arrested and put into jail. Five days later he appeared on a charge of being 'an idle, lewd, and dissolute person'. The lawyer who tried to plead for him was told by the judge, 'these men are wanton, all of them, young or old ... these pleadings ... have not affected me one iota'. The purge went on. More and more men were arrested, among them one of the city's leading physicians, who promptly killed himself. Finally the situation became so embarrassing to all concerned that the crusade was dropped [93]. But such crusades are bound to cause tragedy.

Mass purges of homosexuals are uncommon in England. The Wolfenden Committee found no evidence of witch-hunting on a national scale. Usually the police confine their activities to indecency in public places, to 'cleaning up' bars that become homosexual resorts, and to dealing with men who interfere with children. But sometimes a whole group of men are prosecuted. For example, in July 1954, twenty-eight men came before the Birmingham Assizes on charges of homosexuality. The judge spoke of 'these disgusting practices which corrupt the life of the community' and awarded prison sentences totalling thirty-six years. The exposure of the men was reported to have come about through one man giving up to the police an address book containing the names of 213 homosexuals with whom he had associated over a period of years.[1] Such proceedings, or the threat of them, have been responsible for many suicides. When nine men and two youths of seventeen were brought before Evesham

[1] *News of the World*, 1 August 1954.

Magistrates' Court in April 1956 on charges of indecency a
defending solicitor commented that three others who might
have been before the Court were facing a higher tribunal.[1]
Following questioning one man had gassed himself and
another, a married man with three children, lay down on a
railway line and was killed. Of those actually summoned one
old man of eighty-one was taken to hospital with cerebral
haemorrhage before a verdict could be given. Mostly these
incidents escape public attention because suicides evade
Court appearance. Sometimes a short notice of an inquest
indicates what has happened, as for instance when it was
reported that two men, aged sixty-six and forty-one, gassed
themselves in their home following police inquiries about
indecency.[2] Early in 1958, following some public correspondence about large-scale arrests in Wells, the Homosexual
Law Reform Society was established in order to press for a
change in the law and in particular implementation of the
Wolfenden recommendations. The Society has an impressive list of distinguished supporters.

Some men will run immense risk to satisfy their sexual
drive. In 1953, in England, a detective who had served twenty
years in the police force was sent to prison for indecency in
a Turkish bath. The man had gone to the baths and committed indiscretions there knowing full well that others had
been arrested in the same place by police officers who spied
on the occupants through peepholes.[3]

As there are so many homosexuals in the community it
follows that any large organization will have some among its
members. Thus, after an agitation by opponents of the Tru-
man régime, who alleged that the United States Government was employing perverts, it was announced that ninety-
one homosexuals had been discovered in the State Department and had been dismissed. Whether they were really
security risks, or whether they were political scapegoats is a
matter of opinion. The homosexual writer D. W. Cory, in his

1. *Evesham Standard*, 13 April 1956.
2. *Daily Telegraph*, 16 December 1958.
3. *News of the World*, 19 July 1953.

book *The Homosexual in America,* describes how it sometimes happens in the United States that witnesses in important political court cases are trailed by government
agents looking for irrelevant sex offences with which to in-
timidate them and so discredit their evidence [35]. Altogether, male homosexuals form a very vulnerable minority,
though nothing that has happened recently in Britain or the
United States can compare with the ferocity of Hitler's
bloody purges of alleged homosexuals during the Nazi
domination of Germany.

2. LEGAL ATTITUDES

The attitude taken to homosexuality and the laws relating
to it vary widely from one country to another. Some communities are so tolerant that no social problem arises.
Among Asiatic peoples not only does homosexuality appear
very common but in many places in the East, even today,
it is accepted perfectly casually as a part of life. The typical
Oriental finds in homosexuality an additional sexual outlet
without any particular emotional fixation. He is expected to
marry and to beget children, but beyond that what he does
for his own pleasure is of little significance, and it is not up
to the women to question the ways of their men-folk. Under
such circumstances the men's approach to homosexual practices is playful, their escapades may be exciting and sensual,
but they lack the emotional and disruptive consequences so
often associated with similar affairs in our own community.

On the continent of Europe there is a slightly different
attitude from what is usual in Britain and the United States.
In the Mediterranean countries, at least until recent years,
there was an unselfconscious attitude to male friendships.
In Italy and Greece, for example, girls were carefully se-
questered before marriage and young men were much thrown
together. Strong attachments and open gestures of affection
between young men passed without comment, although
similar behaviour in Britain would lead to arrest. People
were just unconcerned. The Northern Europeans, however,
are usually more selfconscious and critical. Although in

some countries homosexuals have their own officially recognized clubs and are tolerated up to a point, they are nevertheless regarded as odd and would not be accepted everywhere. In Britain, though many individuals express liberal views, the community as a whole treats perverts with hatred and contempt and the law labels them criminal. In Britain, intimacies between men are under all circumstances legal offences, and the homosexual man takes a grave risk if he writes an affectionately-worded letter to a man friend.

The laws governing sex conduct descend directly from ancient religious codes. In ancient times Jewish religious institutions included the *kadesh* or male homosexual temple prostitute (see II Kings xxiii. 7). In the earliest Jewish codes, therefore, and in Hittite and Chaldean writings, homosexuality is condemned only in special circumstances, for instance between blood relations. Horror of homosexual temptation is exemplified in the biblical story of the curse Ham brought upon himself through catching sight of his father, Noah, lying naked in his tent (Genesis ix). After their return from exile in Egypt the Jews came to regard all homosexual practices as foreign, pagan, and idolatrous. In Leviticus xx. 3 it is stated categorically that 'if a man lie with mankind as with womankind, both of them have committed an abomination: they shall surely be put to death'. The Old Testament makes no mention of lesbianism, but St Paul (Romans i. 26) condemns women who lust after one another and give themselves up to vile passions [9].

The Christian Church adopted the ancient Jewish sex codes and formalized them into the Ecclesiastical Laws that governed medieval Europe and later provided the basis for English Common Law. In medieval times, when clerical preoccupation with sins of the flesh was at its height and sexual pleasure of any kind was considered almost damnable, many men and also a few women were sent to their deaths for homosexual offences. Even married persons were not immune from religious investigation, for confessors were supplied with manuals instructing them in questions to be addressed to married couples to ensure that sexual intercourse took place only in the approved position. Sexual perversions must have flourished in this repressive atmosphere, for the so-called penitential books of the period describe at great length and in the utmost detail every conceivable sexual aberration and give appropriate penalties for each sin [184].

In England homosexual offences did not become a matter for the secular courts until 1533 when a statute was introduced (25 Henry VIII c. 6) making sodomy punishable by death. So it remained until the nineteenth century when, under the reforming influence of Sir Robert Peel, the maximum penalty was reduced to life imprisonment. The relevant statute, the Offences Against the Person Act of 1861 (24 & 25 Victoriae, c. 100) covers such crimes as rape and sexual assault. Section 61 of the Act reads: 'Whoever shall be convicted of the abominable Crime of Buggery, committed either with mankind or with any Animal, shall be liable, at the Discretion of the Court, to be kept in Penal Servitude for Life or for any term not less than Ten Years.'

Section 62 of the Act states: 'Whoever shall attempt to commit the said abominable Crime, or shall be guilty of any Assault with Intent to commit the same, or any indecent Assault on any Male Person, shall be guilty of a misdemeanour and being convicted thereof shall be liable, at the Discretion of the Court, to be kept in Penal Servitude for any Term not exceeding Ten Years and not less than Three Years, or to be imprisoned for any Term not exceeding Two Years, with or without Hard Labour.'

Penal servitude and hard labour have been abolished, but the terms of imprisonment remain.

The fact that English law classifies sodomy as a felony means that any citizen who knows of such an offence, or knows that such an offence is likely to be committed, has a legal duty to apprehend the guilty persons and notify the police – a technical detail perhaps, but one that could be invoked in special circumstances. A case in point occurred on 27 August 1954, when a Juvenile Court strongly criticized Coventry Corporation Children's Committee for failing to report to the police offences known by them to have taken place between three boys aged fourteen. The chairman of the bench of magistrates said: 'The city council has been wrong: If felony, or what may be felony, has occurred then it is the duty of all persons who have knowledge thereof to report their knowledge to the Chief Constable.' In this case the reason given by the local authority for not reporting the crime was that they did not want the boys sent to an approved school because they thought that the offences might well be repeated in such a school. Now a large number of sexual felonies come to the notice of the staffs of psychological clinics and are recorded on their files. To do their legal duty the clinics should denounce their patients to the police. The Wolfenden Report mentions this legal point [198] and comments that it may cause some homosexuals to feel reluctant to confide in a doctor.

English law concerned itself only with sodomy and indecency in public until the year 1885 when a Bill was introduced 'to make further provision for the protection of women and girls' and for 'the suppression of brothels'. Henry Labouchère, M.P., moved the introduction of a new clause making indecent acts between males in public or in private a criminal offence. Another Member asked if it was in order to introduce into the Bill an alien topic. The Speaker ruled that it was up to the House to decide, and the new clause was accordingly accepted without any discussion. From then on all sexual acts between male persons, including oral contacts and masturbation as well as sodomy, and regardless of whether they were committed in public or private or between consenting adults, became criminal offences punishable by two years' imprisonment under the Criminal Law Amendment Act of 1885. The change in the law thus unobtrusively introduced did not pass without comment. One Recorder at the time called it scathingly 'the blackmailers' charter'.

Since the introduction of the Sexual Offences Act of 1956, the crimes of buggery, attempted buggery, indecent assault on males, gross indecency between males, and soliciting or importuning in a public place for immoral purposes, have all been brought together under separate clauses of the same Act. But the definitions of the offences and the penalties involved remain unchanged. Consent to sexual activity cannot be given legally by a person under sixteen, and in charges of indecent assault on persons of either sex under that age the indecent act itself constitutes an assault regardless of whether the victim resists or encourages the offender. Homosexual offences comprise a substantial section of British criminal statistics. In England and Wales in the year 1955, 428 men were convicted of buggery, 1,081 of indecent assault on males (including attempted buggery), 995 of gross indecency, and a further 477 men were found guilty of persistent soliciting or importuning.

It is commonly assumed that homosexual conduct between women is not unlawful in England, and prosecutions do not take place in practice; but it might be possible to bring a charge of indecent assault on a female, since the statute does not specify the sex of the offender.

Generally speaking, in countries where the penal system derives originally from British Law, homosexual practices between males are in all circumstances a criminal offence. This applies, for example, in India, in many British colonies, and in the United States. By contrast, in France and most continental countries, and in other places, such as Egypt, where the laws are derived from the Code Napoléon, sexual acts between consenting adult males in private are not illegal.

In the United States the law varies slightly from one state to another. The statutes are variously worded as against buggery, sodomy, crimes against nature, indecent behaviour, perverse acts, unnatural offences, and so forth. In practice there are penalties for all kinds of homosexual acts and in most states the penalties may be as severe as those for serious crimes of violence. Generally the statutory penalty for homosexual sodomy is a long term of imprisonment. In Georgia it is life imprisonment, in a few states it is only one or two years' imprisonment, and in New Hampshire, Vermont, and the District of Columbia the crime receives no specific mention in the statutes [156, 172]. Although the American laws are sometimes so worded as to apply to either sex, in practice, as in England, only males are prosecuted. Kinsey commented that 'in New York City we find three arrests of females in the last ten years, but all of these cases were dismissed, although there were some tens of thousands of arrests and convictions of males charged with homosexual activity in that same period of time [112].'

In France the law makes no specific mention of homosexual acts, which, in theory, are punishable only when they violate laws equally applicable to ordinary sex activities. Thus homosexuals can be prosecuted for public indecency ('*un outrage public à la pudeur*' – Art. 330, Code Pénal) or for corrupting youth ('*attenté aux mœurs, en excitant, favourisant ou facilitant habituellement la débauche ou la corruption de la jeunesse de l'un ou de l'autre sexe au-dessous de l'âge de vingt ans*' – Art. 334). The Scandinavian countries likewise do not discriminate against homosexuals in law, but in Germany and Austria homosexual acts are statutory offences. In Germany, in 1927, a draft code was proposed making homosexual acts illegal only under certain aggravating circumstances, such as corruption of the young or prostitution. A completely opposite course was taken in the Nazi Act of June 1935, by which all homosexual acts became punishable by imprisonment, which was increased up to ten years if any of the aggravating circumstances enumerated in the draft code was present. Austrian law is almost unique in making specific mention of female as well as of male homosexuality. Most legal systems, including the British, tacitly ignore the existence of lesbianism. The Swiss Penal Code (Art. 194) makes provision against the exploitation for homosexual purposes of employees or other dependent persons. In Denmark the Courts are empowered to order the castration of a man who persistently interferes with children, but this law is not specifically directed at homosexuals. In Norway, homosexual intercourse between adult males is legally impermissible, but in practice prosecutions are rare unless young persons are abused. The 1953 Report of the Norwegian Penal Code Commission proposed the abolition of the law against homosexuality, and at the same time drafted provisions to protect young people up to twenty-one against seduction [4].

The 1926 Penal Code of post-revolutionary Russia made no reference to homosexuality, but as in the case of divorce and abortion the law has since become more stringent. In March 1934 a Soviet decree was issued, without public discussion, instructing the republics of the U.S.S.R. to add to their codes an article making sex acts between males an offence. Homosexuality was designated a 'social crime', on a par with such crimes as banditism, sabotage, espionage, and counter-revolutionary activity, to be punished in lighter cases by three to five years' imprisonment (Art. 154 of the Criminal Code) [134].

Oriental countries have hardly passed any laws relating to homosexuality, but in the ancient Muslim religious code sodomy and adultery are serious offences and this tradition has doubtless influenced the civic codes in some places (see *The Koran*, Chapter iv, v. 20 for a specific condemnation of homosexual acts).

In the absence of any comparable figures it is impossible to say whether legal proscription has any effect on the numbers of practising homosexuals. More is heard about the homosexual problem in Germany, Britain, and the United States than in most other countries, yet all three have strict laws against it. Perhaps it is just because of these laws, and the consequent scandal and publicity attaching to detected homosexuals, that the problem looms so large in these countries. Another factor may be the puritanical tradition. A nation so sensitive that it feels the need of legal protection against adult homosexuality is likely to be sensitive also to the developing sexuality of its children. Such a community probably harbours the repressive attitudes that sicken youngsters against awakening sex and thus foster the development of perversions. In the discussion that comes later on the causes of perversion it will be explained how, paradoxically, the more energetically a society strives to force everyone into the strait-jacket of a rigid sex code, the more likely it is to produce aberrant individuals.

The letter of the law does not always reflect the feeling of a community. In Holland and Denmark, where homosexuals have legal toleration and are permitted to meet each other unmolested in recognized clubs, many make no use of the facilities because they fear to shock their families or to lose their professional reputations [110]. In contrast, some sections of society preserve a tolerant attitude regardless of the law. This applies to theatrical circles almost everywhere. In England an actor convicted of a homosexual offence can pursue his career without interruption, but a lawyer, doctor, or clergyman under similar circumstances would be ruined. Homosexuals naturally gravitate to those circles where they are more or less accepted. This may be one reason for the seemingly large number of noticeable homosexuals among musicians, designers, actors, and men in personal service occupations. One undesirable consequence is that where homosexuals gravitate normal men shy away, so that certain types of employment become dominated by cliques of sexual deviants.

3. CHRISTIAN ATTITUDES

Whatever some sections of society may feel, or however tolerant the law may become, Christian dogma pronounces categorically that homosexual practices in any shape or form are morally wrong. Dr Fisher, Archbishop of Canterbury, writing in the *Diocesan Notes* for November 1953 (reported in *The Times*, 25 November 1953), made the following declaration:

'Let it be understood that homosexual indulgence is a shameful vice and a grievous sin from which deliverance is to be sought by every means.'

The Bishop of Rochester, writing for the *Practitioner*, April 1954), explains that 'Christianity reveals ... that complete fulfilment of personality can only be attained when the sexes express the love divinely born in them, according

to the will of God.' He further states that 'homosexual practice is always a grievous sin and perversion. Defective sexual
intercourse between two persons of the same sex can only
be gross indecency under the guise of expressing affection.
Even if safeguards could eliminate the corruption of youth,
and the practice be confined to inverts of mature age, it
would remain the perversion of a wholesome instinct to an
unnatural and loathsome end. For all such inverts continence is demanded.'

The Church does not condemn persons for experiencing
homosexual feelings, for these are beyond the individual's
control, but to give way to the temptation to indulge such
inclinations is considered sinful. The Roman Catholic
Church teaches plainly that all sexual activity is sinful
except that which takes place between man and wife for the
purpose of procreating children.

Until recently the Church has been generally understood
to consider homosexual indulgence a particularly serious
sin, much worse than fornication or adultery. However, in
February 1954 the Church of England Moral Welfare
Council issued a pamphlet, *The Problem of Homosexuality*,
putting forward a more moderate view. The pamphlet, which
was reviewed by *The Times* and other papers, pointed out
that homosexual indulgence is not, as a rule, so far-reaching
and devastating in its third-party consequences as ordinary
pre-marital or extra-marital sexual relations. It recommended that the state, which does not interfere with the
private acts of consenting adults in these latter cases, should
cease to do so in the case of homosexuality. The authors
thought the control of adult homosexuality a matter more
appropriate for the individual conscience than for statutory
legislation. Furthermore, they expressed the hope that informed opinion would make itself heard on the question, as
there was a danger that sensational and prejudiced reports
in certain sections of the press might inflame the public to
the point of demanding persecution as well as prosecution.
In advocating legal reform they emphasized the anomalies
in British law as it now stands. The law ignores lesbian acts,

but punishes men severely. A male importuner may be imprisoned for two years as a 'rogue and vagabond' under the Vagrancy Act. Before the introduction of the Street Offences Act of 1959, a woman prostitute soliciting on the streets received a maximum penalty of a £2 fine.

The recommendations of this Anglican group find a parallel in the views of an eminent French Roman Catholic writer, Father Marc Oraison, a doctor of both medicine and theology. His book, *Christian Life and Problems of Sexuality*, published under the patronage of the Conférences Laenec, and with the Imprimatur from Monsignor Brot, can be taken as an authoritative Roman Catholic viewpoint.[1] Father Oraison shows himself well aware of the secret dramas and personal suffering occasioned by homosexuality, suffering that presents a particularly vivid instance of the general problem of evil. He knows that homosexuals are too readily looked upon as dangerous monsters condemned from the start to eternal damnation, but he thinks such attitudes arise from stupid ignorance and are contrary to elementary Christian charity. He is, moreover, thoroughly opposed to the imprisonment of homosexuals. On the matter of gravity of homosexual sin he writes (p. 250): *'En toute logique la faute n'étant pas formellement mortelle, mais bien de la faiblesse, il n'y a pas de raison théologique valable pour exiger qu'un homosexuel se confesse après chaque défaillance . . .'* [2] [152].

So, in spite of the religious dogma that homosexual acts are always sinful, many responsible Christians are coming to the view that, apart from the protection of children, the law has no business to interfere.

1. Since this was written, Rome has placed the book on the Index. This dismissal of a work that had appeared under seemingly unimpeachable French Catholic auspices caused a commentator in *Le Monde* to ask whether the Elder Daughter of the Church had become the Enfant Terrible.

2. 'Logically speaking, the offence not being officially a mortal one, but rather a matter of weakness, there is no valid theological reason to insist that a homosexual should go to Confession after every lapse. . .'

4. IMPRISONMENT

The question of how far homosexuality should be tolerated
cannot be properly considered until after the causes of the
condition have been discussed. One point, however, can be
made now. Though moral or legal justification may be found
for punishment, imprisonment under present conditions
seems a most unsatisfactory way of dealing with the problem. Confinement in gaol embitters the individual victim
without reforming him and, moreover, serves to spread
homosexual habits among men who might otherwise not
indulge in them [36, 109]. Many authorities have spoken
against the system of incarcerating sex offenders. Judge
Tudor Rees, who was chairman at the 1953 annual magistrates' meeting of Surrey County, said:

'In my view, except for the removal of the corrupting influence,
prison is not the answer to the problem. To lock up in solitary
confinement for eighteen hours out of twenty-four a man convicted of an unnatural offence is to do him far more harm than
good. In the innumerable hours that he has to spend alone he
quite naturally contemplates those very things that he ought to
be encouraged to forget.
'I have had talks with governors and medical officers of
prisons, and with probation officers and others, and I am sure
that, instead of reforming the offender, a prison sentence aggravates the cause of the trouble, and so inevitably leads him into
further mischief when he leaves prison.' (See *The Times*, 8 Dec.
1953).

Prison officials find homosexuals a great nuisance. Their
flirting manners and passing of 'love' notes undermine discipline. Furthermore, fiercely possessive relationships develop in the restricted prison community which lead to violent quarrels and jealousies. Efforts are made to segregate
the obvious 'pansies', but the more secretive ones, those who
do not 'look the type', can never be completely weeded out.
One of the frankest and most disturbing accounts of the
effect of imprisonment is a book entitled *Sex in Prison*, by
J. F. Fishman, one-time Inspector of Prisons to the United

States Government [55]. In this work he explains how the impersonal discipline with no outlet for affection, the bar on all contact with women, the enforced idleness, the perpetual salacious talk, the loss of self-respect and normal standards, all conspire to lead prisoners into homosexual habits. As one ex-prisoner put it: 'To the man dying of hunger and thirst it makes little difference that the available food and water are tainted. Likewise it makes no difference to the average prisoner that the only means of sexual gratification are abnormal' [148]. Ernst Toller, a German dramatist, remarks in the introduction to Fishman's book that in the German prison where he was incarcerated 'Men, who were so conditioned that previously they condemned the slightest deviation from the norm of sexual activity, became homosexuals.'

To some prisoners the awakening of sexual feeling for other inmates comes to them as a horrible surprise and they may for a long time fight against it and try to give no outward sign [22]. But the prison atmosphere creates sexual tension. Men who were homosexual before they came to prison, especially the 'pansy' street nuisances who so often find their way to gaol, aggravate the situation by proffering themselves shamelessly to all and sundry. Good-looking young men find they can take advantage of the situation and gain money or favours in return for sex. They may not at first do this for pleasure, but the habit soon grows into a need. The active type of homosexual tends to 'court' any newcomer who takes his fancy, pursuing his object with the frightful pertinacity of one who has literally nothing else to think about. If the newcomer cannot be seduced by ingratiating tactics he may take to threats. Fishman quotes one prisoner who described how he had been forced into sodomy at the point of a knife. A youth molested by an 'old lag' has, unfortunately, no redress. He dare not give away the offender for fear of reprisals. The whole prison population bands together to make life hell for any inmate suspected of being a 'stool pigeon'. Fishman refers to the numerous allegations by prisoners that they have been forced into sexual practices by warders, and he thinks it quite possible that some of their statements are true. Some individuals may take on the job of prison guard, just as some become 'rubbers' in Turkish baths, for the opportunities of intimacies with men. After repeated debauchings in prison a youth may lose all desire for women.

Nearly every modern book on prisons mentions the homosexual problem. L. W. Fox remarks: 'The problems of homosexuality in prisons are patent to all familiar with prison life.' He then goes on to discuss the possibility of controlled concubinage for prisoners as an antidote to homosexual influences [60]. Books by ex-prisoners often describe most vividly the impact of the homosexual prison atmosphere on hitherto sexually normal men. One such recent work, by Anthony Heckstall-Smith, devotes two most instructive chapters to this topic [175]. He paints a dismal picture of the sexual habits of youths in Borstal Institutions, and gives some account of the mass orgies that take place in confined dormitories. He believes that prison experience turns some youths into male prostitutes. The same problem occurs also in women's prisons, and 'Joan Henry' mentions the matter in her description of life in Holloway [96].

Most of this behaviour in prison arises from the sheer lust of sex-starved men who stop at nothing. As Wilde put it:

> The vilest deeds, like poison weeds,
> Bloom well in prison-air;
> It is only what is good in Man
> That wastes and withers there.

Nevertheless, in prison as elsewhere, the sentiment of love sometimes shows through all the vileness, so that even the hardened criminal will sometimes be solicitous and tender towards the man who gives him sexual affection.

By no means all prisoners partake in homosexual activities. Some preserve a stern self-discipline and an absolute hatred of 'queers'. But the average prisoner does not care one way or the other. Though he may laugh at the effeminate 'pansy' boys, the fellows who chase young men, the

'wolves' as they are called, he never really thinks of homosexuals. Because they do not look or behave unmanly he
doesn't regard them as abnormal.

A flare-up of homosexual behaviour during imprisonment
is not peculiar to criminals; exactly the same happens in
prisoner-of-war camps, as G. Westwood describes in an
account of conditions in Japanese and German prison camps
[193]. In these camps a minority of confirmed homosexuals
would take the chance to run riot and provoke large numbers of 'normals' to indulge with them. Many of the men,
while professing hostility to all forms of homosexuality, had
secret 'affairs' of their own, most of which sooner or later
became common knowledge owing to the lack of privacy.
According to Westwood, after an initial battle the majority
ultimately succumbed to the temptation. He gives several
illustrative sexual histories of interned men. One of these, a
young R.A.F. officer, was captured when he was twenty-one.
He had had no previous feelings of the sort that he could
remember. Men had approached him, but he had always
kept aloof. In the German prison camps he had plenty of
advances, from guards as well as prisoners, but he never gave
way. He had a particular friend with whom he spent most
of his time. One day he found himself admiring his friend's
body, and felt very ashamed and angry, but could do nothing to banish the thoughts. He reached such a pitch that he
could not bear his friend out of his sight. Then one day he
let the friend kiss him. 'It wasn't just a way of relieving ourselves as it seemed to be with most of the others. I can't really
explain it. All I can say is that I have never seen a girl and
a boy who love each other more than we do' (p. 54). On return
to civilian life this man, though he wanted a family and
children, went to live with his friend because they could not
bear to be separated.

A reversal as complete and permanent as this is unusual.
In a study of the effect of imprisonment, Greco and Wright
concluded that, in general, only those sensitized to seduction by previous experience or prior emotional bias became
permanent deviants as a result of experience in prison [81].

Most men regain an interest in women after their release, although some remain confused and disturbed sexually for a long time. The R.A.F. man of this case noticed a crucial point. He and his friend were emotionally involved with each other to a greater degree than most of the other men who similarly indulged. Those who really fall in love in the prison situation are liable to have greater difficulties later on than those who merely play with each other as a change from masturbation.

One can understand the bitterness of individuals who have served a prison sentence for homosexuality. If they were not aware of it before, prison life gives a practical demonstration of how many men take to homosexuality when it suits them, in spite of their protestation to the contrary. The convicted homosexual feels he has been made a scapegoat for behaviour for which thousands of others go unpunished. On his release, when he finds himself snubbed by friends and rejected by employers, his outlook on society comes close to that of the confirmed criminal. Notwithstanding his 'vice' he may not have been a really vicious personality before, but he is likely to become one as a result of experience in and after prison.

5. THE 'MENACE' TO YOUTH

One reason for the public demand for the imprisonment of male homosexuals is the general belief that they constitute a great menace to children. Practically every other case reported in the newspapers concerns the alleged seduction of a boy or youth. This gives a false impression. The police take action much more readily where interference with children is concerned, which accounts for the high proportion of this type of case before the Courts; but there is no clear evidence that homosexuals are more prone than heterosexuals to molest children. The great majority have no sexual interest in children whatsoever. Youths are a different matter. Many find lads of seventeen or eighteen very attractive, but then many normal men are interested in girls of the same age group. Young people in their late teens may not have reached years of discretion, but sexually they are fully mature. A youth should certainly be protected from being led into homosexual habits by the persuasion or bribery of older men, such as occurs in prison; but at the same time it should be made plain that many youths know perfectly well what form of sexual pleasure they want, and may well take the initiative in homosexual advances. Indeed, some unscrupulous youths exploit their ability to tempt older men, knowing full well that if they are caught the older man gets the brunt of the blame.

The little available information about men sexually attracted to children (infantophiles, child molesters) comes from the clinical impressions of psychiatrists. Exhibitionists (men who derive pleasure from displaying their genitals in front of another person) not infrequently perform in front of children, but usually they choose girls. The great majority of homosexuals, like the great majority of heterosexuals, have hardly any interest or curiosity in connexion with sexually immature children. Sexual passion directed predominantly to pre-pubertal children, either of the same or of the opposite sex, occurs relatively rarely, and sufferers from this perversion frequently have obviously immature or damaged personalities, which is not the case with homosexuals. Whereas the ordinary homosexual makes friendly contact with others similarly inclined in order to satisfy his needs, the sexual habits of child molesters are necessarily divorced from their ordinary lives. Sometimes child molesters put up a façade of unusual respectability and sexual purity, only half admitting their real interests even to themselves. But when acting out their impulses, or planning future opportunities for doing so, they show a reckless disregard for danger, and a complete indifference to the harm they may be doing, that contrasts markedly with their generally mild and circumspect characters. One finds men with several convictions for offences against children still volunteering for posts in youth clubs and Sunday schools and being accepted on account of their thoroughly respectable demeanour.

One needs a test to identify infantophiles, and Dr Freund of Prague has developed a beautifully direct method [69]. Using an instrument for registering small volume changes in the penis, Dr Freund found that the responses of a series of male patients to the sight of pictures of male and female nudes of different ages reliably distinguished between homosexuals and heterosexuals and also between men attracted primarily to adults and those attracted primarily to children. In addition to their consistent preference for the same or the opposite sex, the majority of subjects tested also showed a consistent preference for adults, adolescents, or children. Of both the homosexuals and the heterosexuals only a small minority preferred children, but those who did were consistent in their reactions.

Sexual interference with children may cause harm, though perhaps not in quite the way many persons imagine. If a grown man makes sexual approaches to a small boy, there is no reason to suppose the boy will thereby become per-verted. Psychiatric follow-up studies of individuals who, as children, have had sexual experiences with adults, do not show any directly adverse effect upon later sexual develop-ment [15, 161]. Precocious sexual indulgence provides no guide to future tendencies. In an extensive follow-up study of 108 juvenile sex offenders (without convictions for other types of offence) Doshay found no single instance of a known sex violation in adult life [46]. Sexual stimulation of the young is not in itself so harmful. In some perfectly happy primitive communities grown-ups fondle the children's genitals as we might stroke their hair. The children seem-ingly enjoy it and suffer no ill-effects. Nearer home, it is not unknown for a nursemaid to soothe an infant to sleep by tickling its genitals. The harm comes when a child who has been always scrupulously shielded from sexual contacts suddenly finds himself confronted by a powerful adult be-having in a quite new and terrifying manner. Rather than stimulating perverse interests the experience will more likely inhibit the child's sexual inclinations. Still more harm may come about if the parents react with visible horror when

they hear what has happened and insist on the child appear-
ing before a magistrate to testify. From the child's point of
view, an isolated instance of sexual approach by man or
woman is best played down and forgotten as soon as possible. Repeated stimulation by a nurse or relative is a more
serious matter. The child may learn to enjoy and respond to
whatever method is used, and this may well influence his
sexual preferences later on. Moreover the adult's guilty fur-
tiveness will communicate itself forcibly to the child and set
up additional emotional complications.

The frequency of cases of male teachers, choirmasters, and
scout leaders discovered touching boys in their charge probably arises from several causes. The sex segregation and the
increasing sexual tension and curiosity of growing boys
makes them ready to indulge in any form of sexual play.
The man in charge may be the type of homosexual who has
fought shy of overt practices and tried strenuously to 'sub-
limate' his impulses by engaging in youth work. His own
sexual tensions being therefore very considerable, he is
specially prone to give way on sudden impulse. The homosexual who has accepted his condition philosophically and
found an outlet with other adults is most unlikely either to
interest himself in young boys or to be tempted to interfere
with them. Sometimes, however, it is an old man who, because he can no longer find any other outlet, starts to take
an interest in children. But this is not a peculiarly homosexual phenomenon.

5

Two Typical Cases

BEFORE discussing in the abstract some of the varied
theories of sexual deviation, it would be well to have a picture in mind of some actual instances of individuals who
have failed to conform to normal standards. A study of
such cases helps to show how aberrant tendencies develop,
and provides a background against which to judge the
plausibility or otherwise of the commoner explanations.
Here, then, are the personal histories of two homosexual
men, both very typical of their kind.

CASE I

The first example is a person known to me outside the
patient-doctor relationship, an architect by profession, who
agreed to answer my questions for interest's sake. He was
not seeking psychiatric help; in fact he would be the last
person to consider himself ill or in need of treatment. In this
respect he provides a good example of the type of homosexual the psycho-analyst rarely sees because they do not
come for treatment.

He was of medium build, slightly thickset, with a manly
face and body, rather muscular considering his sedentary
habits, and with normal genitals. He dressed carelessly and
one would never notice him particularly in a crowd. In
fact the keynote of his personality was ordinariness. He
avoided sports, walking, and exertion generally, more from
laziness and lack of interest than special aversion, but liked
swimming, which he did well. Though not brilliant in his
profession, he was successful by dint of a capacity for persistent application coupled with considerable practical
ability. Outside his own technical sphere he had few intellectual interests. He held naïve views on political affairs and

questions of philosophy or religion failed to interest him. His approach to life savoured of rather earthy common sense. He knew how to look after his own interests, was even a little egocentric, but more from absense of imagination than lack of goodwill. His disposition was placid and he co-operated with his colleagues easily. They looked upon him as a steady, dependable chap, calm, efficient, and business-like. They would have been greatly surprised to hear about his unorthodox sexual life.

His family background was equally unremarkable. He came from a typical upper-working-class provincial home. His father, one of a large family, had known real poverty in his earlier days. His mother, too, had not had an easy life. She had been reared by a domineering mother and then left to fend for herself at an early age. She was an attractive woman, cheerful, energetic, and sociable. Many men had taken an interest in her, but ultimately she married a man much older than herself, a weedy, anxious type of distinctly retiring disposition. She had inherited something of her mother's strong will and soon she became the dominant partner in the marriage. She it was who made the family decisions, looked after the finances, arranged the holidays, and punished the children when necessary. She it was who saw to it that her son worked hard, visited his school to make sure all was going well, and urged him on until he won a scholarship.

He could not remember having any preference for one or other parent when he was tiny, although his father used to make a fuss of him, taking him on his lap to read to him. By the time he was ten, he felt more drawn to his mother. It was clear to him that she was the real boss and that his father was content that it should be so. He grew rather contemptuous of his father's weak character, and this attitude persisted into adulthood. His father seemed to him limited in outlook and lacking in understanding and he confided more easily in his mother.

As far back as he could remember he had always had some curiosity about sex, but he could not remember ever being interested in girls. The only exception he recalled was an incident at the age of six when he and a small girl showed each other their private parts. He vaguely remembered that even before that he had got some erotic pleasure from a game they played together. The only woman he had ever had a real fondness for was his mother. At school he picked up sex information from obscene drawings and talk and also by reading. He listened to dirty jokes, but was neither specially interested nor specially revolted by them.

It was as early as seven years of age that he first found himself attracted to another boy, one slightly older than himself. He found the boy's company very pleasurable and used to wonder what he would look like undressed. When he was about eleven he remembers there was mild sex play between the boys at school in which they poked at each other's privates. He used to like this being done to him. When he was alone he tried various ways of pleasurable stimulation, but it was not until he was thirteen that he discovered by experiment how to obtain orgasm by regular masturbation. Thereafter he indulged frequently, but he did not feel guilty or worry about its effects because, about this time, his mother lent him a book on sex. On one occasion his father caught him masturbating and warned him that it would make him ill. He could not believe this, and the incident only made him more disillusioned with his father.

At first his masturbation was no more than a bodily manipulation, but around the age of fifteen he suddenly found he could increase his pleasurable excitement by imagining naked men, or looking at photographs of male nudes. Many of his school-fellows indulged in mutual masturbation, and he used to get erections and orgasms by watching them, but he refrained from joining in himself, because his particular friend said it was a nasty practice. As he grew older and his friends talked a lot about girls he remained uninterested. He was not frightened of girls; he just did not bother to seek them out. He had no desire to see girls undressed, but he was very excited by the sight of men with athletic bodies at the swimming baths.

During his later school years, and during his period of
national service, he continued to masturbate to the accompaniment of homosexual fantasies, but he made no actual
contacts with other men. From reading about homosexuality
he gathered that he would never be able to marry, and at
first this thought worried him. He also read about sodomy,
and was disgusted at the thought of it. It was not until he
was twenty-two, when someone in a crowd made advances to
him, that he first went with another man. They had mutual
masturbation in a secluded spot, and it was brought home
to him that there were plenty of other men who wanted the
same thing as he did. During the ensuing years, however,
while he was pursuing his studies, he had only occasional
furtive contact with men he met in public places. In the
course of these clandestine adventures he was initiated into
the practice of *fellatio* and he learnt to obtain great pleasure
from taking the passive role in sodomy.

After some four years of these casual encounters, during
which he never went with the same man more than once or
twice, he met someone older than himself to whom he was
attracted mentally as well as physically. 'Anthony', the man
in question, was a fastidious, mannered *poseur*, artistically
inclined and over-emotional, full of neurotic symptoms, in
fact very close to the ordinary man's picture of a male homosexual. At their second meeting Anthony swore eternal love.
Anthony introduced him to homosexual circles and they
went about together to shows and 'gay' parties. By the time
he had finished his studies, however, he had tired of
Anthony. Thereafter he made friends with one homosexual
after another, each 'affair' lasting only a few months. He
thrived on being chased by some ardent lover, whom he
would encourage up to a point, while being at pains to assert his independence. At the same time he spent a large
part of his leisure hours in bars and meeting places where
he could be sure of finding men like himself, and became
exceedingly promiscuous. He maintained that he did not
want to belong to anyone, he was out for a good time. It was
nice to have homosexual friends, but too exclusive a relation-

ship with one person led to jealousies and scenes, and he would have none of it.

Despite his promiscuity, he longed secretly to find some-one with whom he could have a love relationship as complete and stable as a happy marriage between man and woman. Eventually he met someone better suited to him in age and temperament than Anthony had been, and the two of them began to live together and organize their lives as one, just like any married couple. His attitude changed abruptly, his promiscuous wanderings ceased, his life became more ordered, he took a new interest in clothes, meals, and domes-ticity, he saved money to make a home for the two of them, and declared his firm resolve to make the arrangement last.

Throughout these developments X pursued his work as usual. He liked his colleagues well enough, but most of them were engaged in settling down and rearing families, and he made no intimate friends among them because their per-sonal interests were different. At ordinary social events he felt rather shy and out of things and distinctly bored. This was not noticeable to casual acquaintances, but it was suffi-cient to keep him away from much of the normal com-munity life. He did not feel deprived, for he preferred to spend his time in the company of fellow homosexuals with whom he could be his natural self.

In women's company he was quite at ease in formal and professional situations, but quickly shied away from any amorous approaches. At the mention of having sexual rela-tions with a woman he gave a little humorous shudder. His only real female friend was his mother. For her he preserved a great fondness, taking her out to the theatre and visiting her regularly after he left home. The two of them would joke together as familiarly as companions of the same age. 'We two are so alike,' he said. 'She understands me and knows what I am going to say almost before I have spoken.' He admitted that there was a noticeable lessening in his feelings towards his mother at those times when he was in-volved in passionate affairs with men. He knew about the psychological theory that male homosexuality arises from mother fixation, but he did not seriously think that this had much relevance to his own case. However, after a discussion of his behaviour towards his mother and its contrast with his attitude to his father, he developed a violent headache.

He agreed that if there were some magic treatment that would change him into a heterosexual overnight he would no longer want to have it. All his friends and interests were homosexual, and the idea of a wife and children left him cold. Of course, he said, if he were heterosexual he might feel differently.

Apart from his sexual habits he was a well-adjusted person and showed no signs of neurotic conflict. From his point of view the only problem arose from the legal and social condemnation that forced him to live secretively in order to avoid the prying suspicions of neighbours. Consciously, at least, he displayed no guilt, and did not consider he was doing wrong to live, as he would put it, according to his nature. It brought harm to nobody and he would not mind explaining to any understanding person how he felt about it. Hence this case history.

CASE II

Now, in contrast, a second case. Unlike the first, who accepted the situation with no trouble at all, this man engaged in a constant struggle with himself. He came before medical scrutiny at the age of thirty years, when he went to his doctor and complained of a tired feeling, aching pains in his muscles, poor appetite, and insomnia. He also suffered from moods of depression when he felt no interest in anything and spent all his time moping indoors. Eight years ago he had had an illness involving muscular pain, and for no obvious reasons he had been suffering from similar pains ever since. The doctor sent him to a psychiatrist. At the first interview he revealed that his indulgence in homosexual practices was worrying him terribly. He thought it very wicked, but he could not stop himself. He was deeply ashamed and not at all sure he had done the right thing in telling his guilty secret. He confessed to a vague fear that the hospital case histories might be subject to inspection by some high official of the National Health Service, and that he would be prevented from obtaining decent employment in future.

He was a quiet-spoken man, of medium build, with a normal masculine body and genitals. He displayed no effeminate mannerisms. He had fair intelligence, but self-blame and a deep feeling of inferiority had brought him to a pitiable position. For some five years he had held a steady job as a skilled worker. Although there was never any complaint about his work, he lacked confidence in himself and was always wondering whether he was doing as well as the next chap. Then he did a period of national service as a private. He liked physical training and assault courses, but he panicked on being selected for clerical training, because he feared he would not be able to cope with memory work. At his own request he secured a transfer to something else, but still he was unsure of himself. Fear of doing the wrong thing haunted him, especially when there were other men around. He dreaded what others would think of him if he made some stupid mistake. His pains returned worse than ever and he slept badly. Finally an army psychiatrist saw him and he was discharged as psycho-neurotic.

After this he drifted from job to job, taking on simple, menial tasks that would make no demands upon him, and becoming quickly miserable and bored in each one. He had applied for better jobs, but sometimes he failed to turn up for interview, and sometimes, after having got so far as to be accepted, he backed out on account of last-minute fears that he would prove a failure and show himself up. He would have liked to do an interesting job of some social value, but he felt it would be wrong for him to try for anything decent. In any sort of public work he might be found out and bring disgrace all round. Although he held strong religious convictions, and would have liked to take part in the social life of his church, he kept away because, as he said, it would be a mockery of religion for a homosexual to attend a church.

Although very different in his attitudes from the first case, there were points of similarity in his personal history. He too had been mother's favourite, and described her as kind, understanding, and his best friend. He used to stay in with her of an evening and not feel the need of other company. She had been a strongly-built, vigorous woman who could get her own way without domineering. She had brought up her family strictly and competently, but when her son was twenty years of age she died suddenly. It was at this point that he first lapsed into homosexual habits.

Whatever environmental influences may have caused his homosexual development, they did not seem to have affected his brothers. His elder brother, a happy-go-lucky type who always got what he wanted out of life, was already married and raising a family, and his younger brother seemed likely to be married before long.

As with many male homosexuals, his relations with his father were somewhat odd. His father was a healthy, care-free man, who had held the same job for forty years. He admired his father in some things, and wished he himself were half so steady, but he never felt at ease with him. He complained that his father had never taken much interest in him, never found time to attend his school functions as other parents did. He thought that his father preferred his elder brother to himself, and he remembered particularly that when first he began to complain of nervous troubles his father remarked unsympathetically, 'You're weaker than I thought you were.' After his mother's death his father took up with another woman. He disapproved strongly and left home when the father remarried.

About his childhood sexual feelings he could recall very little. (No doubt he had repressed a great deal.) He said that as a boy he had been completely ignorant and innocent, and was greatly troubled by the obscene talk at school. Although he was nervous, afraid of the dark, and a nail-biter, he thought that his early childhood was happy. But at the age of eleven, he failed in a scholarship examination that he had expected to pass, and after that everything went wrong. The teacher told him there was no reason why he should have done so badly. The failure upset him terribly and, for the first time, he began to feel helpless and to become awkward in everything he tried to do. Bit by bit he dropped out of school activities and lost all his friends. It was to this disappointment at the age of eleven that he traced back all his present troubles.

Owing to an accident in early childhood he had a somewhat crooked nose. On reaching adolescence he became extremely sensitive about this, especially in the presence of girls. His embarrassment about it made him so clumsy and self-conscious that he had to give up an attempt to learn to dance. Even after his nose was put right by an operation the embarrassment persisted. Moreover, he could not outgrow his childhood disgust of sex, and heartily wished that such horrid desires did not exist. The crude conversation of his workmates revolted him. When he was sixteen another youth introduced him to masturbation, and thereafter he indulged himself in solitude while thinking about girls. He feared having anything to do with girls except in imagination in case he made one pregnant. He thought that about the most terrible thing that could happen. He remembered very vividly his mother, who had old-fashioned ideas about sex, saying that she would feel like killing any son of hers who got a girl into trouble.

After his mother's death he took to spending time in bars where he encountered groups of homosexuals. In their company he felt more at ease because he thought they would be less critical of him than normal men. Soon he was indulging in illicit sex, but not without many qualms and inhibitions. He always let the other man make the first advances. He hated another man to kiss or fondle him, he disliked having to masturbate another person, and he would never agree to *fellatio* or to be the passive partner in sodomy. His preference was for the active role in sodomy, but he liked it to take place in the dark as then he felt less ashamed. He made it a rule never to meet his sexual partners a second time. He had only one permanent male friend, of whom he was very fond, but they had ceased having sexual relations after their first encounter. The reason he gave for having relations with men was not that he preferred them but that in so doing he avoided the dread of pregnancy that assailed him when he approached a woman.

In point of fact, he did have a girl friend with whom he went about off and on for over five years, but they never had sexual intercourse and never became engaged. This girl liked to cuddle him in doorways, and on these occasions, when he felt her body pressed against his, he would become sexually aroused, but then his panic fears of pregnancy would overcome him, and he would have to hurry away. Quite apart from this phobia about pregnancy, the idea of intercourse before marriage seemed to him utterly wrong. On the other hand, he feared to marry in case his homosexual tendencies should get the better of him, forcing him to return to his old haunts and be unfaithful to his wife. 'What should I do?' he asked. 'Should I take the plunge, forget everything, and get married?'

Part 2

CAUSE AND CURE

6

Glands and Heredity

I. HORMONE THEORIES

No progress can be made in the search for an understanding of causes without first recognizing that homo-erotic propensities are a part of man's natural biological inheritance. In our culture such tendencies are suppressed, just as incestuous feelings have to be suppressed. It is really remarkable that so many people do succeed in developing exclusively heterosexual inclinations and in losing all recollection of ever having had contrary feelings. The capacity for homo-erotic responsiveness is not, however, completely eradicated; it remains dormant, and can awaken given special circumstances, such as life in prison, in spite of all the individual's efforts to control it. This applies to the average normal person and calls for no special explanation. Adolescent experiences at boarding schools and occasional homosexual incidents in later life, especially if they are provoked by deprivation of customary outlets or the importunate behaviour of a friend, have no pathological significance. Real abnormality is in question when homo-eroticism predominates and the individual cannot enjoy normal relations with the opposite sex.

It is a popular belief that the development of exclusive homosexuality, especially if it occurs in the man of effeminate physique or temperament, is the result of an inborn constitutional anomaly, probably connected with some malfunction of the sex glands, and possibly hereditary [12]. This hypothetical inborn homosexuality, often referred to as true inversion, is thought to be analogous to the masculine behaviour that can be artificially induced in some female animals by injecting sex hormone. The theory of 'true inversion' finds favour with some homosexuals because it releases them from all sense of responsibility. If the explanation of their condition lies in the way their glands work, then no one can expect them to be able to change. In the opinion of the present writer, however, the glandular theory of inversion has little to commend it. In order to weigh up the pros and cons of the matter some basic facts about sex development must first be made clear; and I hope that those familiar with endocrine physiology will excuse these preliminary explanations.

It has been known since ancient times that castrating a young male animal changes its whole appearance and behaviour and causes permanent sterility. Only relatively recently has it been discovered how these effects come about. The testes in males and the ovaries in females, besides producing the sperm cells and egg cells essential for reproduction, also secrete substances known as hormones which circulate in the blood stream. The presence of these hormones has a profound effect both on the development of the bodily features that distinguish the two sexes and upon the development of sexual responses.

The glands which secret hormones into the blood, known collectively as the endocrine system or ductless glands, include the pituitary, at the base of the brain, the thyroid, in the neck, the pancreas, and the two adrenals, as well as the ovaries or testes. Hormones do not exclusively relate to sex development; they influence practically all the bodily processes, acting as chemical governors for the maintenance of equilibrium and the regulation of the speed of physiological changes, and inducing appropriate adjustments of gear when the body is subjected to unusual stress.

The endocrine glands act in unison, the hormones of one gland having a considerable effect upon the activities of the others. The anterior part of the pituitary gland secretes a hormone that promotes sexual development, chiefly by stimulating the activities of the testes or ovaries. Conversely, the ovaries or testes, if they secrete an excess of their particular hormones, cause a reduction in the activity of the pituitary. The pituitary has been called the master gland, 'the leader of the endocrine orchestra', but in reality all the glands function in complex inter-relationship.

All sorts of serious symptoms may be caused by mal-functioning of the endocrine system. The disturbances are usually more extreme if the defect appears before the individual is fully grown. The baby with a thyroid insufficiency develops into a feeble, stunted, pot-bellied, gaping-mouthed, idiotic cretin, but if the hormone he lacks is replaced artificially he may grow quite normally. In an adult, thyroid insufficiency causes thickened, dried skin, falling hair and eyebrows, slow slurred speech, and mental deterioration.

Endocrine disturbances that affect sexual characteristics naturally cause the greatest havoc when they occur before puberty. A castrated boy grows into a eunuch; his penis remains small, his body hair sparse, and his skin smooth; he may not have to shave, his voice is high-pitched, and his figure peculiarly plump without being really feminine. The type is well known in history from the custom of castrating boys for various purposes, such as initiation to priestly cults, to preserve a high singing voice, or to provide slaves to guard harems. The type is also well exemplified in domestic animals, such as the large, sleek, lazy, 'doctored' cat, the tractable gelding, and the plump, hen-like capon.

Testicular insufficiency may occur spontaneously without outside interference owing to disease or mal-development of the testes. In such cases the deficiency in internal secretions shows itself in obvious physical signs. The development of secondary sexual characteristics, which normally takes place rapidly at the age of puberty, is seriously retarded. If the deficiency is extreme and is not treated with testosterone (the principal 'male' hormone produced by the normal testis) the unfortunate youth becomes typically eunuchoid, with high-pitched voice, beardless chin, and ugly, pseudo-feminine distribution of fat on breasts and hips in place of the normal lean, muscular, athletic appearance of the well-developed, healthy young male. In addition, the genitals may remain small and infantile in appearance and seriously defective in function. These bodily signs of testicular insufficiency are accompanied by deficiency in normal sexual feeling. At puberty, instead of having erections, becoming sexually excited, and wanting to masturbate, the eunuchoid boy is impotent and lacking in sexual desire. These deficiencies may be increased by psychological inhibitions due to awareness of bodily inferiority.

The role of the sex hormones in stimulating the development of normal desire has often been demonstrated. For example, in some experiments on a young male medical student, who had only infrequent erections and could not ejaculate, Hamilton showed that injections of testosterone propionate increased the student's sexual desire and enabled him to have normal intercourse with a woman. The injections had to be continued, otherwise the effect wore off, and injections of an inactive substance, which the student believed was the hormone, had no effect either psychologically or physiologically [89]. Clearly, the development of manly appearance, the functions of erection and ejaculation, and the acquirement of robust sexual desires depend in part upon the presence in the blood of an adequate supply of the male hormone testosterone. They depend, of course, upon many other things as well. A boy or girl may remain completely infantile through a fault in the pituitary.

The hormones that hasten pubertal changes in boys are called androgens, the corresponding female hormones are oestrogens. Not all oestrogens come from the ovaries nor all androgens from the testes. Some of the complex hormones secreted by the adrenal cortex, which is present in both sexes, are androgens. Female blood normally contains a considerable amount of androgen and likewise male blood has some oestrogen. This observation leads to an attractively simple theory according to which deviant sex behaviour arises from an imbalance of androgens and oestrogens. The male homosexual supposedly suffers from too little androgen or too much oestrogen and so tends towards female sex behaviour.

If this theory were true one would expect to be able to

demonstrate the faulty hormonal distribution by direct tests
on homosexuals. Further, one would expect to cure homosexuality by making good the deficient hormone with injections. Lastly, one might expect to produce homosexuality artificially by giving oestrogens to men or androgens to women.
None of these expectations is fulfilled in practice [181].

First, the point about the measurement of hormone levels
in homosexuals. Before 1935 it was not possible to determine
the amounts of naturally occurring androgens by direct
chemical analysis, and they had to be estimated by rather
cumbersome biological tests. For instance, the concentration
of male hormone in a given sample might be gauged by
finding out how much of it was needed to restore normal
appearance to an average-sized castrated cock. Such crude
methods are still in use for the estimation of oestrogens.
Consequently our knowledge in this field is not very advanced; but nevertheless the broad outline of the hormonal
differences between the sexes has been demonstrated.

As large samples are needed, and androgens and oestrogens are both excreted through the kidney, estimations in
humans have mostly been based on twenty-four-hour collec-
tions of urine. The measurements show a discernible general
trend in spite of wide variations between individuals. At the
age of puberty there is a quite sudden rise in urinary
oestrogen in the female, from an average of about forty
International Units per day to two or three hundred. In the
male the oestrogen level stays at around forty. The urinary
androgen also increases at puberty, reaching about twenty-
five Units per day in the male and sixteen or so in the
female. Kinsey points out that the rise in androgen and
oestrogen output at puberty cannot be precisely correlated
with the development of sexual desire, since it is males who
have the most notable upsurge of sexual impulses at puberty,
whereas it is females who show the more marked rise in
hormone concentration.

Various investigators have sought direct evidence of
endocrine abnormality by estimating the hormone levels in
the urine of samples of male homosexuals and comparing

the results with similar estimates carried out with normal men. Some investigators have reported no measurable difference [8, 171], but others have claimed that there is a lowering of the androgen-oestrogen ratio in homosexuals [76, 145, 201]. The views of these latter investigators have been severely criticized [146, 165]. The relationship they claimed was in the nature of a statistical correlation that only revealed itself when sufficient cases were examined. They could not assert from the estimations on any particular man whether or no he was homosexual. They failed to make sufficient allowance for differences due to the inaccuracy of their methods of estimation or to the wide variations in hormone levels found in normal persons. In consequence they put forward conclusions based on differences between small samples that might have been mere chance fluctuations [111].

Even had the investigators proved the point that there was a significant lowering of the androgen-oestrogen ratio in the groups they tested, still they would not have established that it was due to homosexuality *per se*. In most endocrine investigations the method of selecting homosexual cases has been rather unsatisfactory. The usual sources are mental hospitals and prisons, but men so chosen may well be suffering from other abnormalities. Moreover some mental illnesses, particularly the schizophrenias, are believed to be sometimes accompanied by endocrine insufficiencies. A lowered androgen-oestrogen ratio in a group of hospitalized homosexuals might be the consequence of a host of other factors apart from homosexuality.[1]

[1] The interpretation of 'androgen-oestrogen' ratios is hedged round with many more difficulties than have been mentioned. The chemical and biological assays of androgens are not strictly comparable. The chemical methods evaluate the amounts of active androgens together with other ketosteroid compounds that are not biologically potent. For the purpose of male-female comparisons it is the testicular function that needs to be explored, but urinary estimations do not distinguish between androgens from the adrenals and androgens from the testes. Furthermore, urinary excretion may not reflect at all accurately the hormonal balance in the blood and tissues. Owing to all these limitations the present methods of investigating hormone balance could only be expected to detect gross disorders.

The invention of paper chromatography, a marvellously delicate method of estimating minute traces of complex chemical substances, may soon lead to big advances in our knowledge of hormones. Perhaps new factors will be discovered that are more specifically 'male' or 'female' than any of the androgens or oestrogens so far isolated. However, as far as present knowledge goes, it would certainly be fair to state that no convincing relationship between hormone estimations and homosexuality has been demonstrated. That is not really surprising, for endocrine abnormalities are relatively rare and they are usually accompanied by physical signs, whereas homosexuality is an exceedingly common condition that presents no recognizable physical stigmata.

To return to the second method of testing the endocrine explanation, namely the administration of male hormone, it can safely be said, in spite of occasional claims to the contrary [129], that as a method of inducing 'masculine' desires this simply does not work. Androgens have a tonic effect on men whose sexual powers are weak or failing. They have been used in the treatment of male sterility, they have a temporary 'rejuvenation' effect sometimes in the elderly, and they can definitely bring about an increase of sexual responsiveness. When given to male homosexuals, however, androgens, far from having a curative effect, are likely to increase the individual's desire for whatever type of sexual activity he is accustomed to [11]. The effect is not invariable. Out of eleven cases so treated by Glass and Johnson they noted an increased drive towards homosexual behaviour in only five [77].

The third approach, the administration of oestrogens to men and androgens to women, likewise fails to bear out the supposed connexion between male and female hormone and male and female desire. The effect of large doses of androgens on women is well known as a result of the naturally occurring adrenal tumours, which secrete large amounts of androgens, and also because big doses of androgens have been given as treatment in certain cancers. The woman's

appearance undergoes a striking change in the direction of
masculinity. The voice deepens, a beard grows, breasts
regress, clitoris enlarges, features coarsen, and feminine fat
disappears. Sexual desire usually increases, but remains
normal feminine desire, unless of course lesbian inclinations
were already present [59, 82, 136]. Correspondingly large
doses of stilboestrol (synthetic oestrogen) have been given
to men in the treatment of cancer of the prostate gland.
Far from inducing homosexual desires, oestrogen simply
brings about a reduction of libido. If continued with for
long enough and in sufficient doses oestrogens destroy
testicular tissue and thus have the same effect as castration.
This fact has been made use of in the treatment of sex
offenders. Stilboestrol sometimes effectively quells desire
and so helps the homosexual to control his behaviour
[47, 57, 80].

Stilboestrol treatment, like castration, is not invariably
successful in abolishing sexual feeling [86]. It also has unfortunate side effects, such as the stimulation of feminine
breast development, which is both painful and embarrassing
[47]. Moreover the ethical justification for interfering with
the little-understood endocrine balance of a physically
healthy man might be called into question. Taking stilboestrol as a 'cure' for homosexuality is rather like 'treating'
a paralysed leg by amputation. However, if a man earnestly
desires this pseudo-castration as a possible escape from
conflict with the law, then one can hardly withhold it from
him. But the effects of castrating an adult male are variable.
When a fully mature young man has his testes destroyed,
as sometimes happens through wounding or tubercular
infection, eunuchoid bodily changes may not occur at all or
may be quite slight. The effect on sexual desire is inconstant.
The Romans knew very well that even eunuchs were not
always to be trusted with women. Although castration of
an adult often causes his sexual desires to diminish, in
some cases it appears to make no appreciable difference.
Some castrated adults continue an active sexual life, although they are sterile. The nervous reflexes governing

erection and ejaculation, once established, can continue unimpaired in spite of considerable hormone deficiency. Also the androgens from the adrenals still circulate after castration. These facts about the unreliability of castration should be taken into account by those who consider this an appropriate method of dealing with male homosexuals.

To summarize so far, the evidence concerning human sexuality suggests that the development of desire at adolescence and the strength of desire in adult life partly depend on hormone secretions, but that the choice of a male or female as love object bears no demonstrable relation to endocrine activity [144, 155]. The only plausible connexion is in the case of men who are sexually inert owing to endocrine insufficiency. These may, perhaps, be somewhat more likely than normally constituted men to drift into passive homosexuality.

The mistaken idea that sex hormones control the direction of the libido probably arose from observations on animals. The administration of androgens has a dramatic effect on the behaviour of hens. Hen communities are governed by a hierarchical arrangement whereby the most powerful and aggressive hen can peck all the others, the next most powerful can peck all but the one at the top, and so on right down to the most submissive hen who gets pecked by all and can peck none back. But give male hormone to a hen low down in the scale and immediately it begins to climb the ladder until it reaches the very top. Not only this, it becomes aggressively masculine in both appearance and behaviour and makes advances to other hens. Similarly, castrated or femininized male mammals are apt to proffer themselves and be mounted by normal males and, conversely, masculinized females become as aggressive as males and attempt to mount other animals. But such behaviour need not involve a change in the animal's sexual inclinations similar to a change from heterosexuality to homosexuality in humans. In animals, the choice of mounting or being mounted is largely a matter of the relative size, strength, and activity of the participating individuals. A strong passionate female may change places and mount the male if he is insufficiently aggressive, and she may be all the more apt to do so after stimulation with androgens, but this is different from becoming homosexual in the human sense. In any case, whatever the influence of androgens and oestrogens on the behaviour of animals, it is their effect on humans which is of primary concern.

2. A BIOLOGICAL 'ANOMALY'

The fact that no gross abnormality of the sex hormones has so far been found in homosexuals by no means disposes of the possibility that some undiscovered physical abnormality underlies the condition. Some theorists suppose that, although homosexuality manifests only on the psychological plane, nevertheless it is caused by some inherent biological peculiarity, that it is in fact a form of intersexuality. Intersexuals are individuals who cannot be said to belong completely to either sex, though they have some of the physical features of both. Their distressing condition is the result of a breakdown of the normal mechanisms that determine to what sex a baby shall belong. Fortunately this happens rarely. The theory that homosexuality is one form of intersexuality deserves some consideration [159].

We know that in the ordinary way the sex to which an individual will belong is determined at the moment of conception according to which of the two varieties of male sperm cells happens to be the one to fertilize the female egg. If the sperm cell contains the extra female-producing chromosome a girl is conceived, and vice versa. The difference in chromosome inheritance between males and females does not make itself apparent for some time. In the first month or so of life in the womb the growing foetus shows no visible sign of the sex to which it belongs, but thereafter the male and female develop along different lines until at birth they are fully differentiated. Intersexual individuals, however, are not fully differentiated, and may be born with almost every conceivable mixture of male and female sexual features. Many grades of intersexuals have been noted and studied. In some cases the internal sex glands are at variance with the bodily appearance. In some cases the glands are neither ovaries nor testes but a mixture of the two, containing both androgenic and oestrogenic cells. In some cases there is a testis on one side of the body and an ovary on the other. The external genitals may range through every intermediate stage from male to female. Thus an individual with an apparently normal penis may have in the position of the scrotum a small cleft leading to a rudimentary womb. Body build and other external appearances may be equally confusing.

The causes of physical intersexuality are only imperfectly understood. Sometimes an endocrine disorder beginning during foetal life produces intersexuality. A rare example of this is over-activity of the adrenal glands in a foetus of three to four months, causing masculine development of what would otherwise have been a normal female. We have already seen that after birth sex hormones have only limited effects. They may stimulate the development of such secondary sexual characteristics as breasts, hair, and voice quality, and they may keep the genitals infantile or cause them to grow to maximum size, but they cannot change a person's fundamental sex. In the foetus, before the sex organs are fully differentiated, hormone influences can produce much more radical changes. Hens' eggs treated with oestrogens during the first week of incubation hatch into normal females, intersexual monstrosities, and a very reduced proportion of male chicks [70]. In most cases of human intersexuality, the foetal endocrine disorder is itself the result of an inherited factor, a flaw in the chromosome constitution. One relatively common type of intersexuality (male pseudo-hermaphroditism) is a familiar disease transmitted by the mother. The offspring are either normal seeming females or intersexuals – no boys. Apparently these intersexuals are biologically males, but some factor from the mother has brought about a femininization process. Typically they possess male testes, which are in their immature, undescended position, but they also have a rudimentary vagina and womb. On the evidence of the external appearance of their genitals they are likely to be classed as girls, but at puberty a beard, a deepened voice, and other second- ary sexual characteristics typical of the male make their appearance [2, 197].

Arguing from the analogy of these physical intersexuals, Lang has suggested that male homosexuals are really genetic females whose bodies have undergone a complete sex reversal in the direction of masculinity. On this theory it is difficult to explain the normal bodily appearance of the great majority of homosexuals. If their condition were due to a sex-reversing process one would expect to find many cases of incomplete masculinity. However, Lang adduced one curious piece of evidence in favour of his theory. He investigated the family background of 1,517 male homo- sexuals whose names he obtained from a German police register. He found that in the aggregate they had 2,534 brothers but only 2,034 sisters, a male-female ratio of 124 to 100. This figure differed significantly from the male- female ratio for the population as a whole. Seemingly male homosexuality was associated with an excess of boys in the family. The observation fitted in well with Lang's theory. The excess of apparent males would be accounted for if some of them were in fact genetic females whose sexual development had undergone a radical reversal towards masculine appearance [120]. Their sexual preferences, in- stead of being regarded as being perverse, could then be looked upon as the persistence of natural feminine impulses in spite of their bodily masculinization.

Recent work by Pare at Maudsley Hospital has disproved Lang's theory [154]. Fifty homosexual men and fifty con- trols (half men and half women) gave samples of scrapings from the cellular membrane lining their mouths. The cells were examined by modern microscopic methods which per- mit discrimination between male and female sets of chromo- somes by means of observation of the incidence of chromatin spots in the cell nuclei. All 75 men, including the 50 homo- sexuals, were identified as biologically male, and all 25 women as female. Cases may conceivably occur of homo-exual apparent males who are genetically female, but none uch appeared in this series.

The preponderance of brothers in the families of homosexuals might be explained in many ways without accepting Lang's theory of intersexuality. For instance, families of boys might provide more opportunity for homosexual play than mixed families, and this in turn might be associated with a greater likelihood of permanent homosexual tendencies. Then again, families of brothers might be more liable than mixed families to develop aggressive anti-social ways and so to find themselves on the police register used by Lang. One could go on enumerating hypothetical explanations indefinitely, but there is no need because other workers have failed to confirm Lang's factual observations. Darke, in a repeat investigation, found no significant preponderance of brothers in the families of 100 American homosexuals [40].

Instead of confirming the biological theory of homosexuality, studies of human intersexuals afford additional evidence that the direction of the sexual inclinations does not depend upon physical constitution. Despite their bisexual appearance, intersexuals are not necessarily bisexual in their desires. One might expect that their sexual impulses would follow the pattern of their internal sex glands, that those with ovaries would develop feminine inclinations, those with testes masculine inclinations, and those with mixed glands bisexual characteristics. But it does not work out like that. An intersexual's desires are more likely to fall in line with the sex in which he is reared than to conform to the sex to which his endocrine glands belong. Many of them are brought up as boy or girl on the basis of an arbitrary decision made immediately after birth after an inspection of the genitals. Sometimes the decision runs contrary to the true sex as reflected in the internal organs. When this happens upbringing is apt to triumph over the sex glands. Ellis demonstrated this point by abstracting from medical literature all the cases he could find in which an intersexual's glandular constitution and sexual preferences were both known [49]. He found 84 cases distributed as follows:

INTERNAL SEX GLANDS (GONADS)

Reared as –	Male		Female		Mixed		All Types	
	Male	Female	Male	Female	Male	Female	Male	Female
Attracted to men	0	19	0	3	0	11	0	33
Attracted to women	11	2	5	0	18	3	34	5
'Bisexual'	0	1	0	2	0	0	0	3
Immature	0	1	0	1	5	2	5	4
Total	11	23	5	6	23	16	39	45

The table shows that of 39 intersexuals reared as males 3 showed definite sexual desires. In all 34 cases their desire followed the normal male pattern, although 23 of them had either mixed or female sex glands. The inclinations of intersexuals seem, therefore, to correlate more closely with their upbringing than with their hormonal constitution. In a later study of 100 patients with different types of intersexuality Money and Hampson [143] confirm that, with rare exceptions, the psychology of these patients follows the sex of rearing, even in cases in which their chromosomes and the predominant characteristics of their external genitals and their internal reproductive organs are those of the opposite sex. This is strong evidence in favour of the view that heterosexuality and homosexuality are attitudes acquired by psychological conditioning, and against the view that they are pre-ordained by endocrine factors.

3. AN INHERITED FACTOR

Although no physical abnormality has yet been discovered, the assumption that there must be some underlying constitutional defect would receive some support if it could be shown that homosexuality is hereditary. Many difficulties stand in the way of an answer to this question. In the case of some rare and clear-cut defect, like a missing finger, the mere observation of several instances in the same family affords good evidence of a hereditary factor. But homosexuality is so common that the discovery of a number of cases in the same family would have no significance. Even if investigation revealed some families with an unusually high proportion of homosexuals in several successive generations, this still would not amount to proof of hereditary causation. Like infectious disorders, homosexual tendencies might be transmitted by association. A homosexual father's peculiar outlook might so influence his sons that they develop the same way, even though they have no inborn peculiarity and under other circumstances would develop normally. Nor should the possibility of seduction be overlooked. If several brothers are affected, this may be the result, not of hereditary defect, but of one brother having introduced the others into perverse practices. In addition to the difficulties arising from alternative theoretical interpretations, actual data are hard to obtain. The extreme secrecy which surrounds sexual habits, especially within the family circle, makes it almost impossible to secure reliable estimates of the numbers of relatives of homosexuals who have similar tendencies. A voluntary patient would not permit the doctor to ask such questions of his relatives for they, of all people, are the ones from whom he most desires to conceal his sexual deviations. Inquiries among the relatives of convicted persons would scarcely lead to much information for they would naturally be antagonistic and reluctant to make admissions of any kind.

In the teeth of all these difficulties, both practical and theoretical, Kallman, an American authority on human heredity, has achieved a remarkable investigation on male homosexual twins [107, 108]. The study of twins enables the investigator to sort out the effects of hereditary and environmental influences. There are two types of twins. Dizygotic or ordinary twins, produced by the simultaneous fertilization of two separate eggs by two separate sperm cells, are no more alike than ordinary brothers and sisters. Monozygotic or identical twins, supposedly produced by the splitting of a single egg into two shortly after fertilization, descend bot[h] from the same egg cell and sperm cell and so have precisel[y] the same hereditary endowment. Identical twins are alway[s] of the same sex and bear an uncanny resemblance to eac[h] other in general appearance and in such identifying char[-] acteristics as finger-prints and blood groups. Now if [a] particular condition occurs frequently among brothers th[e] explanation might be that it was a hereditary condition[,] but it might also be due to the fact that the brothers had [a] similar upbringing and similar life circumstances. In studie[s] of twins, if it is found that a condition occurs more often in both members of pairs of identical twins than it does in pairs of ordinary twins of the same sex, this affords stron[g] evidence of a hereditary factor. Ordinary twins and identica[l] twins are both brought up in similar environments, but onl[y] the identical twins have the additional factor of precisely similar inheritance.

Kallman naturally experienced some difficulty in securing homosexual men with twin brothers and in following them up once he had found them. He had the cooperation o[f] such organizations as the New York City and the New York State Departments of Correction, but it cannot have been easy. He remarks that this is 'not a promising field o[f] exploration for research workers who are in any way anxious for their conventional peace of mind . . . the problems and attitudes of a sexually aberrant group look less wholesome in the twilight of gloomy hiding places than they do from the perspective of an ornamental desk or from a comfortable therapeutic couch' [83].

In the end he secured 85 homosexually-inclined twins. Most of them were more or less exclusively homosexual[,] that is to say they would be rated 5 or 6 on Kinsey's scale. All of them were at least 3 on the Kinsey scale. Of these 85 40 were identical twins, and of these 40, Kallman succeeded in tracing the brothers of 37. He found that all 37 twin brothers were homosexually inclined (with a Kinsey rating at least 3) and 28 were more or less exclusive homosexuals (with a Kinsey rating 5 or 6).

In striking contrast the brothers of the ordinary, non-identical twins showed no particular homosexual trend. Twenty-six were traced, and only 3 had a Kinsey rating of 3 or more. This represents an incidence no higher than that of the population at large.

There is no gainsaying this dramatically significant difference. The figures suggest a 100 per cent similarity between the homosexual trends of identical twin brothers and no particular connexion between the sex habits of non-identical twin brothers. Even diseases such as schizophrenia, which has long been known to have a strong inherited factor, do not give such perfectly concordant results. (Kallman's corresponding figures for schizophrenia were 86 per cent concordance in the case of identical twins and 15 per cent concordance in ordinary twins.) Taken at their face value the figures seem to imply that heredity alone decides whether a man becomes homosexual and that life experience and upbringing count for nothing. Such an unexpected conclusion cannot be accepted without some reservations.

It would be wrong to put too much reliance on the outcome of one isolated investigation. Kallman's challenging results call for further research and confirmation. In the meantime on the basis of his initial observations only very tentative deductions can be made. That there really is 100 per cent concordance between identical twins in respect of homosexual tendencies seems most doubtful. At least one case has been published of a pair of identical male twins (the brothers 'Otto and Erich Hiersekorn') one of whom was completely heterosexual and the other completely homosexual. Otto was a vain, painfully skittish-mannered homosexual, passive in his sex habits, who had never got pleasure from women. Erich had a girl friend and intended to marry her. About relations with men he declared, 'It disgusts me to think of such a thing' [121]. I myself have come across a pair of seemingly identical twins, one a practising homosexual and the other definitely not, but owing to the usual difficulties the case has not been scientifically investigated. If Kallman had pursued his investigations further no doubt he too would have encountered cases of discordant twins.

Still, the important point is not whether homosexuality is 100 per cent hereditary, but whether or no a substantial hereditary element enters into its causation. Kallman himself does not suppose that homosexuality as such is directly inherited, or that it is necessarily unalterable. He considers rather that the inherited factor renders the individual particularly prone to a homosexual outcome. He compares the situation to the inheritance of right-handedness and left-handedness.[1]

One explanation of Kallman's figures, apart from the inheritance of homosexuality, is that they are due to the temperamental similarity of identical twins, which causes them to react similarly to any environmental influence. If one gives way to homosexual influences then the other will too, not because they have an innate bias in that direction, but because they are both so alike they react similarly. In the case of non-identical twins the situation is different. An overpowering mother, for instance, might drive one son away from women and into homosexuality, while the other son, because he is more strongly constituted than his brother, merely becomes rebellious and aggressive.

If seduction by young boys were an important cause of adult homosexuality one would expect to find evidence of twins contaminating each other regardless of whether they happened to be identical or non-identical. Kallman's findings with regard to the absence of homosexual concordance

1. Kallman's actual words are: 'The most plausible explanation of this finding is that the axis, around which the organization of personality and sex function takes place, is so easily dislocated that the attainment of a maturational balance may be deranged at different developmental stages and by a variety of disturbing mechanisms, the range of which may extend from an unbalanced effect of opposing sex genes to the equivalent of compulsive rigidity in a schizoid personality structure. From a genetic standpoint this multiple causation of overt homosexual behaviour in the adult male as an alternative minus variant in the integrative process of psychosexual maturation is comparable to that of left-handedness in a predominantly right-handed world.'

between non-identical twin brothers are some evidence against the seduction explanation. In the case of the identical twins, Kallman stresses that they all claimed to have started their homosexual practices independently of each other.

One last point about Kallman's investigation. He, like so many other investigators in this field, was forced to draw his cases from among the criminal and the abnormal. Out of his 40 identical twins, one was definitely schizophrenic, and at least 22 were 'definitely schizoid', 'severely unstable with obsessive compulsive features', or else excessively alcoholic. Only 10 were thought to have achieved a sufficient adjustment to life. Any conclusions based on such a group of pathological personalities cannot safely be applied to homosexuals as a whole. It may be true that certain abnormal types are specially liable to homosexual developments – that point is considered later – and it may be true that these abnormal personality traits are hereditary, but it does not follow that homosexuality in general, which is associated with no special personality defect, is also an inherited condition.

7

The Psycho-Analytical Approach: An Introduction

It is no longer seriously disputed that sexual interests begin early in life, and that the emotions lived through during development greatly influence attitudes later on. Though they disagree on matters of detail, psychologists as a body support the view that the origins of many cases of sexual peculiarity can be traced back to childhood. The process of exploration, the delving into the dim recesses of memory to reawaken childhood feelings, is called psycho-analysis. Unfortunately the name arouses prejudice because it stands also for the mass of psychological doctrine, some of it highly suspect and controversial, propounded by followers of the Freudian school. As a method of exploration, however, psycho-analysis has long been vindicated. Even those psychiatrists who are opposed to the more speculative theories, agree that psycho-analytic explorations have brought about a fresh and deeper understanding of human motives and human vagaries.

In this chapter only the bare bones of the psycho-analytic approach need be considered. The higher flights of speculative interpretation, and the controversies on points of detail between the protagonists of different psychological 'schools', are best left to the specialist to argue over. The essentials of our problem can be understood well enough in the light of a few basic concepts that need not strain the credulity very much.

Many of the concepts laboriously formulated by psychoanalysts after prolonged study of the memories and dreams recounted by their patients are really matters of common observation put into technical jargon. The first essential is to recognize, as most people do today, that human behaviour is often impulsive, guided less by rational reflection than by a host of emotional attitudes and tendencies, the strength of which the individual does not fully realize. Only by prolonged rumination and agonizing self-questioning can one gain insight into some of the remote influences that determine conduct and feelings. The analysts call this exploring *unconscious motives*.

In ordinary life we do not go in for introspective searchings. If our motives are questioned, we are apt to *rationalize*, to put forward some reasonable-sounding but spurious justification that did not really occur to us until after we had acted. It is easier to see this happening in other people. Listening to a woman giving vent to her feelings by criticizing a friend for extravagance we may be perfectly sure from her tone of voice that her motive is jealousy, but she herself would be the last to see it, and if challenged she would firmly assert and genuinely believe the rationalization that she was giving helpful advice.

Psycho-analysts have drawn attention to the great extent to which our thinking and acting rests upon these unconscious self-deceptions. They give names to the commoner mental tricks – *repression*, for example. When we are repelled by our own feelings, when they clash with our self-respect, we try to deny or to banish the offending thoughts. Often we are successful, and unwanted, inconvenient memories fade much quicker than pleasant, reassuring ones. The process has its uses. But for the development of a few healthy repressions civilization could not work, for, like wild beasts, we should be the victims of each other's untrammelled murderous impulses. We can deal with the nasty side of our natures in two ways, by repression, or by acceptance plus rational control. We can, for instance, accept the unpleasant fact that we sometimes feel like murdering our relatives without necessarily acting on the impulse. But many find repression the easier solution. Trouble arises when repression has not been complete and the repressed tendencies keep peeping through. This happens particularly in neurotic individuals who have the unfortunate habit of trying to repress too much and too often.

When the effort to repress is strong, but the repressed tendencies will not stay quelled, the individual feels tense and miserable without knowing why. Torn between his conscious wishes and his unconscious, repressed feelings, he is said to be in a state of *neurotic* conflict. The sufferer does not appreciate the nature of the conflict. He feels neurotic symptoms, anxiety, depression, irrational fears, and so forth, but he does not know their origin. The second of the two cases described in Chapter 5, the man who could not associate with women on account of his pregnancy *phobia*, was a typical instance of neurotic conflict. Phobias are the neurotic's danger signals, and they come on most acutely in situations that stimulate partially repressed tendencies. In the case of this young man, for reasons not yet clear but doubtless related to his puritanical attitude to sex, he had tried to repress his desire for women. Confronted by a situation of temptation, in which his desires threatened to get the upper hand, his symptom would appear – a feeling of unbearable tension. The pregnancy scare was just his way of rationalizing his fear and explaining why he ran away from women. His phobia, like most neurotic symptoms, provided a form of escape, a means of retiring from the conflict situation and at the same time drawing attention away from the unpleasant dilemma that was the real cause of the trouble.

Sometimes the real nature of the conflict appears perfectly obvious, at least to outside observers. In wartime, pilots who had been specially selected for their toughness and mental stability nevertheless fell a prey to neurotic symptoms under the enormous strain of long-continued and desperately dangerous duties. The conflict between the partially repressed desire for self-preservation and the urge to fulfil a duty ultimately became intolerable. Without realizing what was happening or why, a man would succumb to obscure ills and depressions. In such cases the element of conflict counts more than the actual danger. Narrow escapes from drowning or the like rarely cause neuroses, but protracted battles between irreconcilable impulses eventually result in breakdown. In experiments with animals the conflict situation can be artificially staged and the process of breakdown watched and studied. The poor beasts are given increasingly complicated choices to make, and for every wrong choice they receive a painful electric shock. The point comes when suddenly the animal breaks down and becomes too trembly and excitable to make even the simplest choice. Again it is the element of conflict and not the severity of the punishment that precipitates the breakdown.

Psycho-analysts contend that problems of love and sex are at the root of most cases of neurotic conflict in humans. Certainly the majority of neurotics seen in civilian life have trouble in their sexual relations. Once food and safety are assured, sexual release and affection become man's most pressing needs, and the two are closely associated. Analysts are at one with poets and romantics in believing that love is the great fount of all human striving. They call it *libido*, a word standing for both the sensual and the spiritual urges of love. Libido is present in infancy. The sensual cuddling and suckling of the infant are the veritable precursors of the passionate embraces of the grown man. Libidinal urges are strong and their manifestations varied, but in the interests of family and social institutions they must be brought under rigorous control. At all costs such inconvenient manifestations as incest and homosexuality must be prevented. The individual must therefore learn to repress if he is not to find himself in a cleft stick. He cannot accept society's standards, including the sense of unutterable disgust for sexual nonconformists, without repressing a great deal of his own instinctive impulses. Unfortunately not everyone succeeds in maintaining a healthy appetite for the legitimate marriage partner, while repressing all socially undesirable tendencies.

Neurotics fail to achieve this adjustment. In an effort to conquer completely all sexual desires of a forbidden nature, they repress too much, and so cannot enjoy uninhibited relations with another person under any circumstances.

Hence impotence, sexual frigidity, guilty feelings, and general *gaucherie* are the prime features of neurosis. The process begins in childhood. The infant possesses libido but lacks adult discrimination. He becomes attached to whoever tends him and, unless restrained, he enjoys himself playing with his own and other persons' bodies. Such behaviour occurs quite openly in societies that make no attempt to suppress their infants' sexual curiosity, but in our community these free and easy ways are usually curbed as soon as they appear, and the child quickly develops a sense of shame that spares his parents' susceptibilities. From then on until puberty he passes through the so-called *latency period*, during which overt sexual behaviour is said to be in abeyance.

The psycho-analytic conception of sexual development agrees with outside evidence in maintaining that the infant's first responses are bisexual. Both boy and girl embrace the mother that suckles them, the question of gender scarcely arises. Heterosexual and homosexual developments come later. A boy of five, however, is old enough to have an acute appreciation of sex differences. He realizes that women have secret, hidden parts to their bodies, and that if he feels fascination or curiosity on the matter he must conceal it from his mother. He knows that he is meant to grow up like father, and he looks forward to the day when he will have the same power and privileges; but meantime he has to play second fiddle, let his father have first place in his mother's affections, and stifle his jealousy as best he can. This stage of development is the notorious *Oedipus Situation,* so named from the legend of Oedipus the foundling who returned as an adult to his native land and unknowingly killed his father and married his own mother. When he found out what he had done remorse made him gouge out his own eyes. Psycho-analysts claim that young children indulge in 'incestuous' fantasies of ousting and replacing the rival parent. When such thoughts appear they arouse intense guilt feelings and fears of punishment, especially punishment by mutilation or castration. Altogether the situation is so unpleasant and frightening that the whole matter is vigorously repressed.

Put so baldly, and in adult vocabulary, this description sounds implausible, but direct observation of children confirms that they do indeed harbour fantasies of the kind. In games like 'fathers and mothers', in scribbled drawings, in dreams, in fact in any situation in which the child's imagination has free play, the theme of Oedipal rivalry with fears of retributive punishment obtains thinly-disguised expression. After a time, however, such is the uncomfortable, guilty flavour of these fantasies, the idea is firmly repressed.

The theory of Oedipal conflict was first propounded by Sigmund Freud from a study of the *free associations* of his neurotic patients. They lay on a couch and let their thoughts flow in a day-dream while the analyst passively recorded what came forth. They were urged to speak aloud and with absolute frankness everything that came to their mind, however personal or unpleasant. In spite of their inhibitions, their thoughts tended to run on to topics that they found most painful. Ideas that ordinarily they would keep repressed would seep through into their reverie, and slowly the conflicts responsible for their symptoms would emerge. Time and time again the Oedipus theme cropped up. Freud did not invent the story; patient after patient related it to him, and such has been the experience of hundreds of analysts ever since.

Confirmation has also come from other sources, from child studies, from researches among primitive tribes, and from observation of psychotics. The ravings of the insane are apt to break the bonds of repression and display in brutal, undisguised form the same incestuous fantasies that the analysts first discovered in neurotics.

The analyst's use of technical terms to describe emotional life gives an exaggerated impression of clarity to the chaotic fantasies with which he deals. Conceptions such as 'incestuous guilt feelings' and 'castration complex' are the analyst's intellectual crystallizations of the general tenor of the patient's half-conscious fears and fancies. In the patient's own mind matters are never so clearly formalized. Incest guilt is not a clear-cut precept derived from formal prohibitions. Normal parents would never talk to their children in such language. Nevertheless, disgust and disapproval in certain contexts are efficiently communicated without verbal instruction. The child senses his parents' unspoken feelings and responds intuitively. In the process, he builds up a fantasy pattern of his own, an unreal, dreamy constellation of emotional ideas. In this private fantasy-world the Oedipus complex takes shape, but it is never verbalized, never conceived in such harsh, unequivocal terms as 'incest' and 'castration' unless an analyst happens to come along and force the patient to consider the meaning of his fantasy.

Normally the Oedipal situation is left behind in childhood, but persons who have experienced a particularly intense parental attachment accompanied by severe guilt feelings may continue for the rest of their lives to try to fight against all sexual responses. In adult life such persons cannot enjoy any sexual relations without conflict because, unconsciously, they continue to associate all sex feeling with the incestuous desires they had to battle against in childhood. They are said to suffer from an Oedipal complex. This complex, or variations of it, accounts for many manifestations of sexual neurosis.

Nothing can so well convey the reality of the Oedipal complex as actual contact with a neurotic sufferer in whom this feature is prominent. A young woman, for example, without in the least realizing what she is doing, may select a man friend resembling her father in a thousand little ways and then, when he makes love to her, she breaks out into a state of acute neurotic tension with all the usual fears and symptoms. The process becomes understandable when the lover is recognized as an unconscious father-substitute with whom sex is impossible.

Frigidity and attachment to a parent-substitute are only two particular examples of the ways in which an unresolved Oedipus complex may manifest. To take another case, a woman may act on the unconscious theme, 'If I can't love father at least I can be like him.' I knew one such person. She suffered from feelings of anxiety and depressed moods that were so severe that she could hardly carry on with her work. Her love life consisted of one long, forlorn attachment to an older man. He had left her years before after a brief flirtation, but she continued to worship him from a distance. She worked at a routine job in a factory. One day she discovered that she had a talent for composing songs. She had no musical training and couldn't even write down the themes that came into her head. What is more, she developed a hoarseness of voice for no discoverable reason which prevented her doing more than hum the tunes. But she flung herself into the business with passionate intensity, and she found a musician who would transcribe and harmonize her inventions. At the same time as all this was going on, she also developed a great fondness for cats, and although she could ill afford to feed them, she took several cats into her home. The inner meaning of her behaviour became clear when it came to light that her father had been a musician who had a great passion for cats. He would have been a singer but for a throat trouble contracted early in his career. He had deserted his family when she was a child and at the height of her emotional attachment to him. Consciously she scorned his memory, but unconsciously she was for ever trying to follow in his footsteps.

Another common manifestation of Oedipal conflict is the man who finds himself impotent with women of his own social set, yet capable of relations with prostitutes. Women at all like his mother are forbidden fruit to him; he shies away from them, or is content to put them on a pedestal of purity. Some mother-fixated men go one stage further and are cold to all women and able to respond only to their own sex. This is the essence of the Freudian interpretation of how homosexuality comes about.

A boy with a too intense and exclusive relationship with his mother develops correspondingly violent guilt feelings and fantasies of punishment by castration. The whole painful constellation of ideas is repressed, and for a time all sexual thoughts are banished, but as the boy grows up and the sexual urges become more insistent the conflict reawakens. He fights shy of any sexual feelings towards women because they are too like the forbidden feelings towards his mother that he was at such pains to repress. He feels no pleasure at the contemplation of the female form. Their lack of male organs suggests castration and stirs up his repressed fears. In his dreams he may visualize the woman's genitals as a dangerous, biting instrument ready to trap and injure him [53].

Fantasies recalled by patients undergoing psycho-analysis provide the chief evidence for these interpretations, but a certain amount of confirmation is to be had from the personal histories of male homosexuals. One point stands out above all others – their unusual attachment to mother. It is nothing out of the ordinary for an adult homosexual to stick to his mother, to take her about with him and fuss over her like a 'best girl'. Inability to come to terms with women of his own age may be one factor contributing to the symbiosis of bachelor son and lively mother, but the process dates right back to childhood days when the intense mother-son relationship first developed. Both the cases given in Chapter V showed the importance of the mother figure in the lives of these homosexuals. The second of the cases brought out this aspect particularly well. The man wanted to be heterosexual, but when he tried to have relations with women he failed because his inner tensions were too great. Memory of his mother's warnings about 'getting a girl into trouble' filled his mind with guilt, and he had to run away. In addition his feelings of unworthiness and inferiority, and his peculiar sensitiveness about his nasal deformity, lend themselves to interpretation as the outward signs of the unconscious fantasy of having been 'castrated' as a punishment for sexual guilt. Sensitiveness about imagined or unimportant deformity and neurotic fears of lack of manliness are characteristic of what the analysts call castration complex. It will be remembered how this man emphasized with shame his father's taunt of many years ago, 'You're weaker than I thought you were.'

Many male homosexuals assert that as far back as ever

hey can remember they have found their own sex attrac-
ive, but never have they had the least interest in women
exually. The theory that their trouble arises from repressed
r inhibited heterosexuality strikes them as absurd. How-
ver, their assertions on this point deserve sceptical treat-
nent; they are on a par with the 'normal' man's assertion
hat never in his whole life has he had the slightest homo-
rotic feeling. Analysts maintain that whenever the mental
ife of a homosexual is thoroughly explored, past hetero-
exual feelings come to light, and vice versa in the case of
eterosexuals. In the first of the cases previously quoted, the
nan was as exclusive an homosexual as ever one would come
cross, but he admitted to one slight experience with a girl
vhen he was very young. Actually, this admission cost him
nore embarrassment than the recital of all his homosexual
dventures.

Granting, as I think we must, that fantastic notions born
of guilt and fear do operate in neurotic minds, it is still an
pen question how important they are as determinants of
omosexuality. Oedipal fantasies have been laid bare in
housands of psychological investigations. Whether a sub-
ect is healthy or neurotic, homosexual or heterosexual, the
ersistent analyst will eventually unearth some traces of
Oedipus conflict. Even when the conflict rages with peculiar
everity, the outcome is not always the same. Some men find
efuge in impotence, some in prostitutes, and some in homo-
exuality. Other factors must come into the picture. The
Oedipal theory explains certain features of sexual develop-
nent, but it by no means tells the whole story.

Apart from the abnormalities already mentioned, of
vhich the commonest are frigidity in women and homo-
exuality in men, a reaction against normal sexual relations
nay show itself in other peculiarities, such as exhibitionism
r fetishism. Exhibitionists derive their sexual pleasure from
xposing their private parts in front of a member of the
pposite sex. Fetishists use personal articles belonging to
he opposite sex, usually pieces of clothing or under-
arments, to excite themselves while masturbating. Traces

of these tendencies may appear in the love play of norma
persons, but they amount to real perversions only when the
constitute the sole methods of obtaining sexual release. Bot]
forms of perversion are usually found in men, and the
clearly represent a form of inhibited heterosexual approach
The exhibitionist has to keep a safe distance from th
woman; the fetichist cannot bear a real woman at all an
contents himself with a harmless, inanimate symbol. A
with other perversions, once the individual has becom
accustomed to respond sexually in a particular situation, hi
pattern becomes strongly conditioned and difficult to alter
In these two perversions the sexual drive is diverted fron
the normal love object to a highly artificial substitute. Th
selection of a lady's shoe, for instance, as the only means o
sexual gratification, is a psychological quirk that cannot have
been inborn. Such extreme examples make it easier to appre
ciate how choice of love object may be determined psycho
logically rather than genetically. The homosexual differ
from these other types of pervert in that his sexual patterr
does involve a close relationship with another person. Thi
encourages emotional maturation, and is partly responsibl
for the fact that many homosexuals achieve a commendabl
personality development in spite of their sexual handicap

8

A Consideration of Psychological Causes

ᴌᴀᴄᴋ of perspective has led some theorists to accept uncriti-
ally their own taboos, to label homosexual impulses un-
atural, and then to search fruitlessly for glandular or
ereditary causes of the supposed abnormality. The Church
as been a step ahead of this in regarding deviant inclina-
ons as just another instance of the many 'evil' impulses
ith which mankind is naturally endowed. But to an ancient
ʃreek it would seem as absurd to call a person wicked as to
ssume he is ill merely because he indulges in homosexual
leasures. Homosexual impulses are only abnormal in rela-
ion to our own standards of correct behaviour. The fact re-
uiring explanation is not the existence of homo-eroticism
ut the inability of a minority to conform with the social
aboo against it. Why is it that the majority are able suc-
essfully to suppress all homosexual feelings while a
ninority, in spite of every possible discouragement, still find
heir own sex the more attractive? The answer to this conun-
Irum may be found in the exploration of psychological
actors [127].

Apart from exploration of individual cases by means of
sycho-analysis, the investigation of psychological causes
ould be tackled most profitably by systematic comparisons
•f groups of persons. The life histories of large numbers of
epresentative homosexuals could be contrasted point by
oint with the histories of a comparable group of hetero-
exuals. One might find a significant preponderance of such
actors as 'dominant mother', 'only child', or 'puritanical
amily' among the homosexual group. Unfortunately this
method, though it could hardly fail to yield most important
nformation, has never been fully exploited. As has already

been pointed out, grave difficulties stand in the way o
assembling and investigating a fair sample of male hom
sexuals. The coordinated efforts of a research team such a
Kinsey's might succeed, but so far psychiatrists have show
no inclination to initiate or research foundations to spor
sor the project. Distaste for the whole business, and the pro
fessional man's fear of compromising his reputation by di
playing too great interest, have had a lot to do with thi
neglect. In consequence, clear scientific evidence as to th
important causative factors is simply not available.

Perusal of psychiatric literature yields nothing more tha
a collection of opinions based, for the most part, on person
observation of a limited number of cases without an
attempt at systematic comparisons with normal groups. Th
psychiatrist notices that a number of homosexual men i
his clinical practice are only sons. He therefore gives out th
opinion – and he may be right – that this is a factor in th
genesis of the condition. But he does not and cannot chec
his impression scientifically, for that would involve a pro
longed and systematic statistical inquiry. Limited experienc
and personal bias affect nearly all psychiatric opinions o
this topic and give rise to the most varied and contradictor
viewpoints. One psychiatrist will assert that in his experienc
seduction plays a major role in homosexual development[48
while another pours scorn upon the same idea. A meticulou
review of the contradictory assertions contained in psychia
tric literature, appropriately labelled with the date an
author's name, might give an impression of studious learn
ing, but it would be a waste of labour. The best one can d
is to give an over-all picture of the more authoritativ
opinions which have gained wide acceptance, and to attemp
a reasonable synthesis taking into account the evidence from
non-psychiatric sources that has already been discussed.

No single causal explanation can possibly cover all cases
All kinds of psychological influences may combine to tip th
scales towards homosexual development, and the factors im
portant in one case may differ radically from those most con
cerned in another. Generalizations true for many cases wil

not apply to all, and interpretations that seem diametrically opposed may be perfectly correct in particular instances. With all these reservations in mind, we can now consider some actual explanations.

2. PERVERSITY: SEDUCTION: SEGREGATION

A consideration of the two case histories given in Chapter 5 serves to dispose of some of the more facile interpretations. Neither case could be accounted for by sheer obstinate perversity. The first man obtained no pleasure whatsoever from contact with women. Heterosexuality meant nothing to him, yet since boyhood he had felt strongly attracted to other males. Over this state of affairs he had absolutely no control, and could no more react potently with a woman than a normal man could react with a cow. Whatever the cause, homo-eroticism was as much a part of him as the colour of his eyes, he could no more change it by an act of will than he could abolish hunger and thirst. The second man's feelings were just as involuntary. Although he had desires for women, heterosexuality was impossible for him on account of the unbearable tension that feminine contacts aroused. The torture of self-reproach occasioned by his puritanical attitude, though a worse punishment than any that might have been legally imposed, was of no avail in changing his inclinations. To call the feelings of persons like these 'perverse' leads to misunderstanding. In common speech a perverse person wilfully chooses the wrong path, but the difficulty of most homosexuals is that they cannot conform however much they might like to do so. Some, indeed, do enter into forced relations with women, and may get married in order to avoid suspicion, or to satisfy the demands of nagging relatives; but all too often the effort leads only to unhappiness, scandal, and divorce.

Seduction, another much over-worked explanation, has hardly any application to cases such as these two. Initiation into overt sexual practices must take place at some stage or other, but that scarcely implies seduction. In the first of the cases quoted, the man was fully mature when first he allowed

a stranger to approach him. His reaction was not, 'Here i
something new', but 'Here is what I have been waiting for'
In the second case, the young man deliberately sought ou
the company of homosexuals because, as he said, with
women absent he felt less tense and self-conscious. In both
cases the preference for other males was well defined before
overt practices began. In these circumstances 'seduction'
means no more than initiation into the various technique
of bodily stimulation.

Factual evidence of the after-effects of homosexual seduc
tion is conspicuously lacking, in spite of strongly held
opinions. Calder, giving 'a prison medical officer's viewpoint'
notes that men in prison for sex offences often complain
bitterly of seduction in youth and say that is what perverted
them [29]. On the other hand Gibbens investigated 100 Bor
stal lads of 16 to 21, asking if any stranger or adult had ever
made a pass at them or tried to interfere with them [73]. O
the lads with known homosexual trends 32 per cent reported
such experiences, of those without known homosexual ten
dencies 33 per cent reported the same experience. The
majority of the lads looked upon the experiences they had
had with older men as trivial and not worth mentioning
when describing their sexual experiences with other youths.

Sometimes, however, the personal history suggests that
seduction may have played a part in a homosexual's de
velopment. A man may date his homo-erotic interests to
some childhood experience when another boy, or perhaps an
older man, first stimulated him sexually. That any such iso
lated incident could be the true reason for permanent homo
sexuality seems most doubtful. Youthful seduction may ex
plain how an individual comes to start overt practices early
in life, but it does not in the least account for heterosexuality
failing to develop. Probably the nearest seduction ever
comes to provoking homosexuality is when it serves to reveal
to unscrupulous youths a means of obtaining pleasure and
material advantage at one and the same time. But seduction
is really no more than an incident on the road. The real
causes of permanent homosexuality lie deeper.

Boys in boarding schools are likely to have their first sexual experiences with other boys, but the frequency of homosexual indulgence at school has probably more to do with the strength of the sex drive than the direction it will take in later life. Kinsey thought that boys reaching puberty early would stand more chance of experiences with other boys and consequently of developing a homosexual orientation. A factual study by Hemphill and others [92] suggests, on the contrary, that homosexuals are relatively late starters as regards overt sexual acts. However, Gibbons found that youths who had been brought up from an early age in institutions were relatively inexperienced heterosexually. One has to remember that segregation in boyhood may cause difficulties in socio-sexual adjustment quite apart from any experience of seduction. C. S. Lewis has described in his autobiography the kind of homosexually orientated culture that can develop among boarding-school boys and produce a harmfully inhibiting effect on heterosexual contacts [123]. The lack of psychological contact with womankind may well be a more important contributing factor than the experience of sexual play in the dormitories.

3. PARENTAL RELATIONSHIPS

Laymen and psychiatrists alike believe that 'mother's boys' risk growing up homosexual, and reports from clinicians who have seen large numbers of homosexuals usually emphasize the frequency of unhealthily intense mother attachments [87]. Neodoma [149] notes that in addition to adoring their mothers many have either no interest in their father or else positively dislike him. While the dominant possessive mother gets most of the blame, some observers, including Anna Freud [61], have pointed out that the weak, unsatisfactory, or absent father forms an important part of the picture [3, 7, 128]. Psycho-analysts stress these points since they fit so well the expectations of the Oedipal theory. In his classic exposition of psycho-analytic theory [53] Fenichel comments: 'The majority of homosexuals not only present an Oedipus love for their mothers, just as do neurotic individuals, but for the most part the intensity of the mother fixation is even more pronounced. Sometimes the devotion to mother is not unconscious at all but frankly talked about.' 'The homosexual man identifies himself with his frustrating mother in one particular respect. Like her he loves men.' The Oedipus situation also involves rivalry and rejection of father. Fenichel goes on to say: 'The probability of a homosexual orientation is increased the more a boy tends to identify with his mother. Children in general tend to identify with the parent from whom they have experienced the most impressive frustrations. This explains Freud's findings that those men are more inclined to become homosexuals who have had a weak father or no father at all, who, in other words, were frustrated in crucial things by their mother.' In a typical case history one finds father a meek, unassertive underdog who lets mother rule the home. Sometimes one finds no father at all; he is dead, divorced, deserted, or gone to gaol. Or else, what amounts to the same thing emotionally, father cuts himself off from his children by an over-stern or aloof attitude. In all these cases mother dominates the children's lives. If, in addition, mother adopts a possessive attitude and keeps her offspring tied to her apron strings, and if it happens she has an only child who has no brother or sister relationships to offset the maternal domination, then the situation becomes that much more acute.

Both the cases described in Chapter 5 conformed to the dominant mother pattern. In the first case father was a weak individual, despised by his son. He kept in the background and let his wife run everything. In the second case father was said to be aloof and unsympathetic, whereas mother was the good friend and stable companion.

In any collection of case histories one finds the same pattern repeated again and again. The first few examples from G. W. Henry's book *Sex Variants* – a valuable source of case histories – serve to illustrate the point. The very first case, Thomas B., happens not to run to type. His father was a violent-tempered, frightening person against whom his mother was passive and defenceless. The second case,

Nathan B., is more typical. His father was extremely puritanical, rigid, and a slave to discipline; he used to strap the children frequently. Nathan was a timid child, afraid of his father, afraid of rough boys, and generally a 'sissy'. His mother was highly strung, but energetic. He was the youngest child and he was petted outrageously by his mother and his elder sister. In the third case, Rodney S., father was an alcoholic, who was garrulous and popular with strangers, but hardly opened his mouth at home. He spent periods away having treatment. Mother was a person of 'charm and breeding' who was affectionate with her son and liberal in her attitude to sex. Rodney began by being unselfconsciously attracted to both sexes, but he had no special ambition for masculinity. He went to work in theatrical circles, and slowly developed a definite preference for relations with other men. The fourth case, Michael D., is classical. He was the only son of a family dominated by women. Mother was a competent business executive who bossed the home. Father was a submissive man often in disgrace in the eyes of his womenfolk. His wife kept him waiting years before it suited her to marry him. His son had scant respect for him. Michael himself was a nervous child, handicapped by bad health, and teased as a 'sissy'. He felt very lonely. He had physical experiences with woman prostitutes, but only men could give him emotional as well as physical satisfaction, and so he slowly developed exclusively homosexual inclinations. In the fifth case, Eric D., father was 'inclined to be quiet' and 'slightly effeminate'. Mother, an ex-school-teacher, was 'mildly domineering' and 'somewhat a matriarch', but she was never demonstrative in her affections. As Eric expressed it: 'I never had any affection and I always wanted it.' Malcolm E., the sixth case, said his father was 'an extremely indifferent sort of man'. Mother 'took the initiative' and saw to the disciplining of the children. She had to urge her husband to give her some support. Malcolm used to help her about the house, much more so than his brother did. Well over half conform to the pattern of absent or unsatisfactory father and a mother who dominates the child's life to an unusual degree. But Henry's examples also show how other factors obtrude in even the most clear-cut instances of mother fixation [93].

So far we have dealt only with personal impressions that might be mistaken. It is arguable that neurotically inclined men of all sorts tend towards mother fixation, and that in this respect homosexuals only follow the general rule because they are neurotic. Two systematic studies on the point have been reported. Jonas [105] put a series of set questions to 60 overt homosexual male patients and to a corresponding number of non-homosexual controls. He found that 43 of the homosexuals stated their unqualified favouring of mother over father, as compared with only 18 of the controls, whereas only one of the controls expressed hatred of father compared with 9 of the homosexuals. In a study based on case histories collected at Maudsley Hospital, West [192] copied out the descriptions of each parent from the notes of 50 overt homosexual patients and 50 non-homosexual neurotic controls. The descriptions were given to an independent judge for rating, who did not know the diagnosis. It was found that a combination of abnormally intense relationship with mother and definitely unsatisfactory relationship with father occurred commonly among the homosexuals but not among the controls.

One must not conclude that all boys who have this pattern of disturbed parental relationships will become homosexual, but it seems to be an important factor. One has here one of the few definite clues to a means of prevention.

4. SEX ROLES

The frequency of this constellation of dominant mother plus unsatisfactory or absent father fits the Freudian theory well, but such a background also implies the presence of other important factors not taken into account in the simple version of the Oedipus situation given in the last chapter. To take one outstanding point, the absence of a satisfactory father figure means that the growing boy lacks an adult masculine hero on whom to model his own behaviour. The process of *identification,* whereby a child adopts as his own the standards and ways of thought of his parents, amounts to much more than deliberate imitation. However he may seem on the surface to battle against parental injunctions, he does in fact absorb most of his parents' habits. If it were not so, cultural characteristics could not be preserved from one generation to the next Children naturally seek the security of parental approval, and in so doing they automatically absorb much of their parents' attitudes, including snobberies and prejudices as well as more wholesome values.

In matters of sex, the boy normally identifies with his father and takes upon himself his father's manly, assertive approach to life. What constitutes the manly ideal depends upon the culture in which one lives. In our society, though customs are changing, the man still retains something of his 'lord and master' role. He is allowed and expected to show more self-assertiveness and adventurousness than the more submissive, demure, and dependent woman.

The 'mother's boy', who has no adequate father figure to emulate and no one to counteract the maternal domination, may suffer ostracism as a sissy because he fails to acquire the toughness expected of a healthy youngster. This in turn may drive him still further away from the conventional masculine outlook, invoke inferiority feelings, and contribute to his difficulties in making contact with girls. The example of a weak, hen-pecked father will certainly not inspire him with confidence in his relations with the opposite sex.

Difficulty in conforming with an uncongenial or too exacting masculine role may be an important factor in some cases. It was pointed out in the first chapter how some primitive communities that make very heavy demands upon their menfolk, in the way of prowess in hunting and warfare, also have a *berdache* system which provides an official homosexual escape for the occasional misfit. Our own society makes less spectacular demands, but all the same the qualities of leadership and the sense of economic responsibility expected of the family man do not suit all temperaments. Moreover, men are supposed to take a lead in all sexual matters, to initiate advances, to show a certain competence. In order to win a desirable mate, the man must arrive at a socially acceptable compromise between the moral dicta regarding continence and chastity and the need to prove his worth as a lover. The young man with too many scruples finds himself at a disadvantage. For some temperaments the task is far from easy.

Dissatisfaction with their sex role occurs most often in women, owing to the fact that our society tends to despise some of the qualities which women are expected to possess. The feminine-mannered homosexual man evokes universal contempt, as if feminization were the worst fate possible. If a masculine group has petty squabbles it earns the reproach, 'You're behaving like a bunch of women.' Jobs with the best pay and the most prestige usually go to men, while the task of looking after the home and children has not quite lost its inferior status. Reaction against an imposed inferiority explains why some women assume an excessive heartiness, take to trousers or tailored suits, and find pleasure in masculine pursuits.

Of course, not all shy men are homosexuals nor all aggressive women lesbians, but the possession of temperamental features contrary to the accepted criteria of masculinity and femininity makes sexual adjustment more difficult. The shy man inclines to run away from women, the aggressive woman finds that men run from her. Such persons may regress to an earlier phase of adolescent homosexuality if their first attempts at heterosexual experience prove too humiliating.

Those who believe that the homosexual trend establishes itself once and for all in infancy, as a result of Oedipal conflicts, find it hard to accept that the young adult's social frustrations can have anything to do with the determination of his sexual orientation. But a predominantly homosexual youth may sometimes overcome his inhibitions (provided they are not too deeply ingrained) through experience with a sympathetic and not too demanding woman, and it seems reasonable that the reverse process may sometimes occur and a potentially heterosexual youth become inhibited as a result of a painful rebuff or an initial failure. Psychologists are coming round more and more to the view that, though emotional trends may become established in childhood, they are susceptible to reinforcement or counteraction by later influences. Admittedly the man who has led an exclusively homosexual life for many years cannot change his ways, but that may be due to the strong conditioning of physical experiences and emotional attachments rather than to the fossilization of reaction patterns in infancy. In fact, when a homosexual succeeds in changing his outlook as a result of psycho-analytic treatment, the change depends as much on the strength of his current motivations as upon his ability to resuscitate and deal with Oedipal guilt.

5. HINDRANCES TO HETEROSEXUAL ADJUSTMENT

Not all male homosexuals are 'mothers' boys'. Freud himself saw that quite different factors operate in some cases. For instance, boys who have lost their mothers may become homosexually orientated through trying to win the affections of the remaining parent by playing the role of substitute wife. Freud suggested that one reason for the prevalence of male homosexuality in ancient Greece was that boys were tended by male slaves. An all-male atmosphere, as in a family of brothers, may have the effect of instilling a sense of hyper-masculinity and a contempt for women's ways that seriously interferes with the development of relations with girls. The sporty 'man's man', who has no time for the petty limitations of domesticity, exemplifies this type.

The one common factor in all these situations is some hindrance to relations with the opposite sex. It may be through Oedipal guilt, it may be through maladroitness or 'sissiness', but whatever the most appropriate interpretation in a particular case it amounts to this: homosexual adaptation occurs when heterosexual adaptation proves too difficult. That is why a too puritanical upbringing can be dangerous. A child instilled with disgust for normal sex is all the more likely to try furtive, substitute outlets. The history of sexual

perverts, homosexuals and otherwise, suggests very strongly
that an overmoralistic upbringing can have a most evil influence. The remorseless progression from sex taboos,
through fear and guilt, to repression and homosexuality,
was clearly shown in the case in the previous chapter of the
man with a pregnancy phobia.

But what of the Oedipus theory? First the case of the pregnancy phobia was treated as an excellent example of Oedipal
guilt, now it is used as a stick to beat the puritans! The contradiction is more apparent than real, for the two interpretations are complementary. A dominant mother fosters
Oedipus conflict, and at the same time her puritanical attitude ensures that the conflict will be accompanied by the
maximum of guilt feeling. Thus in homosexual cases the
Oedipus conflict provides the central theme, but any number of subsidiary themes may appear and contribute to the
total effect. It is essential to read actual analytic case reports
in order to understand the wide variety of emotional
dynamics that can enter into the genesis of homosexuality.
In some cases such factors as inability to cope with the
rivalry of more successful brothers, or intense jealousy of
father, may play a decisive role [116, 122, 163, 170].

To recapitulate a little, the discussion so far has led to the
following tentative conclusions. The available evidence indicates no definite relation to body build or glandular constitution, but suggests a connexion with particular kinds of
upbringing. For instance, the only boy who has a dominating, puritanical mother and no proper father seems specially
prone to homosexual developments. This kind of family
background probably brings about its effect by provoking
Oedipal conflicts and encouraging guilt feelings and sexual
inhibitions. Social ineptitude, shyness, inferiority feelings,
and any other factors tending to interfere still further with
normal sexual contacts, may be expected to aggravate the
situation. Exclusive homosexuality then presents itself as an
alternative adjustment, a half-way refuge for those who find
full adaptation to heterosexual life too difficult. In so far as
the factors of seduction or of segregation of the sexes con-

tribute to the outcome, in most cases they do no more than point the way to the homosexual outlet. Frustration of normal outlets is the primary cause.

Although this seems the most logical explanation, many observers dispute it on the following grounds. If the root cause consists of a neurotic inhibition of normal sexual impulses, one would expect to find glaring neurotic traits in most homosexuals. Some psycho-analysts maintain that this is just what they do find. For instance Bergler writes: 'Homosexuality is an unconscious and trouble-making defence mechanism, and has to be viewed in the same way as other neurotic and trouble-making defence mechanisms' [20]. He goes on to explain that they are sick people and: 'Even if the outer world were to leave them in peace, homosexuals would lead miserable lives.'

Systematic inquiries, such as those by Curran and Parr, Lambert, Liddicoat, and Loeser [39, 117, 125, 126] fail to confirm these impressions and point to a large proportion of apparently non-neurotic homosexuals. Evelyn Hooker [100] applied a series of psychological tests of neurotic tendency to 30 volunteer homosexuals and 30 heterosexuals, matched for age, intelligence, and educational background. The heterosexuals achieved no better 'adjustment scores' than the homosexuals. It will be recalled that the first of the men whose histories were given in Chapter 5 – and he is typical of many – had no obvious neurotic traits and enjoyed his sexual practices without reservation. Neurotic inhibitions are associated with impotence, frigidity, or sexual malaise, but a great many homosexuals display a marked lack of inhibition and love nothing better than a fresh sexual adventure. The answer to this objection is simple. In the process of establishing a homosexual outlook, the original neurotic conflict often burns itself out. Homosexuality has its drawbacks, but at least it provides a workable adaptation to life. The inhibitions of the completely impotent person allow him no release of sexual tension, and so he falls a prey to perpetual nervous frustration and chronic neurotic malaise. The homosexual, on the other hand, does obtain satisfaction, both physical and emotional, and so long as he can bear with social disapproval, he achieves a passable adjustment. Though he has not solved his sexual conflicts in the best possible manner, he has at least arrived at a solution which leaves him free of immediate tension and capable of developing his personality in other directions. The point has been put very clearly by the psychiatrist Dr K. Soddy.

It is not within everyone's power to develop completely, and a small minority of both sexes remain in a state of homosexuality. Nevertheless their emotional adjustment may be stable and secure at the immature level; their physical means of gratification may remain within society's canon of adolescent conduct, and meanwhile the development of other aspects of their character and intellect may proceed normally. When this happens no social evil will result, other than loss to society of potential parents [177].

Provided he accepts his position philosophically and mixes with others of like mind, the homosexual can leave behind the emotional turmoil that originally drove him away from women. Neurotic conflict only remains evident in those who do not fully accept either homosexual or heterosexual adjustment. The man with the pregnancy phobia was like that: he could not face women, nor could he accept homosexuality. As a result his conflict was never stilled and preoccupation with it ruined his work and prevented the maturation of his personality in other respects. His was a case ripe for psychological treatment, whereas the mature homosexual, one who has arrived at a calm outlook and a tolerable way of life, would scarcely be helped by a revival of long-resolved conflicts. In many cases the mature homosexual suffers from his efficiently repressed heterosexuality no more than the mature married man suffers from the complete repression of homosexuality. Explanation in terms of 'burnt out' or 'completely resolved' conflict accounts for the many homosexuals who, though nervous, shy, and inhibited in their younger days, became later in life mature and gifted personalities without ceasing to practise their perversion.

. 'BISEXUALITY'

o far we have only considered cases of exclusive homo-
exuality, which seem fairly evidently the consequence of
nhibitions in relation to the opposite sex; but what of
bisexuality' and 'occasional homosexuality' both of which
re extremely common? In such cases the question of abnor-
nality, psychological or otherwise, does not necessarily arise.
The ancient Greek, the primitive tribesman, and the uninhibited Oriental may all indulge with young men, but in so
loing they only fulfil an impulse that, in their particular
environment, seems quite natural and allowable. In the con-
ext of the beliefs and attitudes of the present day, however,
homosexual practices under any circumstances come under
the shadow of abnormality. Nevertheless, an ability to re-
pond homosexually may merely indicate a failure to develop the strong inhibitions assumed by the majority. In
tself it can hardly be called pathological, and may imply
no more than the possession of a strong sexual appetite that
eeks every possible outlet. Sometimes, however, it is the
symptom of a more serious condition, and betrays an under-
ying weakness of character similar to that which makes
men slaves to alcohol or drugs. The individual who acts out
the boast that he can make use of man, woman, or beast is
likely to be the sort of person who has to satisfy his every
impulse regardless of the consequences to himself or others.
Such intractable rebels against the *mores* of sexual conduct
have much in common with pathological liars, criminals,
and other anti-social types. But this brings us to the relation
between homosexuality and mental abnormality, which is
the subject of the next chapter.

7. LESBIANISM

Before leaving the question of causation, the subject of
female homosexuality calls for some comment, but here one
comes upon difficult ground. Firm conclusions are impossible on account of the extreme scarcity of reliable information. The female problem has been even more neglected

than the male, but the investigations by Katharine Davis, G. V. Hamilton, G. W. Henry, and A. C. Kinsey give some hints on which to build one or two tentative generalizations.

Though common enough, homosexuality occurs less frequently in women than in men. Frigidity is a more prevalent female complaint. It would seem that in response to sexual difficulties women are more prone to react by complete repression and inhibition of all sexual feeling, whereas, other things being equal, men seek substitute outlets. The perversions of fetishism and exhibitionism are virtually limited to males. Kinsey noted one reason for this. Whether through differences in upbringing or differences in biological constitution, men are sexually more labile than women, more easily aroused by the sight of attractive bodies, by salacious thoughts, or by pornography. They are therefore more liable to stimulation by accidental homo-erotic contacts or suggestions, and more prone to seek release through that channel.

Women, on the other hand, are more apt to form emotional attachments to their own sex, which fall short of actual physical practices, though they may exceed in intensity the feelings they have for men. Katharine Davis's investigation showed how very common this tendency is in women. A half of her sample of 1,200 unmarried college graduates reported having intense emotional experiences with other women, whereas only a quarter of them admitted to physical contacts that were recognized as sexual. Although the first sections of this report were not published until about 1920, the material centred on experiences around 1900. Since then the increasing emancipation of women in the expression of sexual inclinations may have somewhat shifted the balance from emotional homosexuality to overt practices, but still the picture differs radically from that of male homosexuality which usually presents itself as a fully recognized physical attraction. Indeed, many promiscuous homosexuals put but little feeling into their adventures, and use the other person primarily as a means of obtaining release from sexual tension. Among lesbians, however, love and physical expression tend to be more closely welded.

Another difference arises from the fact that a man must be fully aroused in order to have sexual intercourse, whereas a woman can remain passive and let the man satisfy himself even though she feels revulsion rather than pleasure. Lesbians, therefore, can and do marry and have intercourse with their husbands in spite of obtaining physical satisfaction only by contacts with other women. Circumstances make it easier for these married lesbians to give up homosexual contacts as they grow older; their male counterparts, who more often remain bachelors, have less motive and less opportunity to change their mode of life.

In spite of these differences in frequency and ways of expression, lesbianism and male homosexuality probably spring from the same roots. In both cases neurotic family background, typified by sexual maladjustment and marital discord, colours most of their personal histories [30, 43, 94]. All the most important factors concerned in the inhibition of heterosexuality – Oedipal conflict, fear of sex, guilty feelings, sense of inferiority – occur in women as well as men. Of the common generalizations made about lesbians compared with male homosexuals it is said that family backgrounds, character, and temperament show more obvious disturbance. Crushes at school on teachers of the same sex, feelings of rejection by the opposite sex on account of ugliness, and painful experiences of attempted heterosexual intercourse are all more frequent in lesbians. They tend to aggressiveness and tomboyishness in childhood, and to ape their fathers, who do nothing to discourage them. They are more likely to experiment heterosexually, and even to marry, possibly because they need not fear impotence. In addition, it is said that lesbians are more likely to be attracted to effeminate men than are homosexuals to boyish women. One psychological characteristic of many lesbians that all observers seem to agree about is rebellion against their sexual status, but as has already been pointed out the inferior position of women in our culture provides a partial explanation of this reaction.

9

Homosexuality and Mental Abnormality

I. NARCISSISTIC FIXATION

THE simple version of the Oedipal conflict outlined in Chapter 7 does less than justice to psycho-analytic theory. Freud worked out the complicated course of developing sexual aberrations in considerably greater detail [62]. He came to the conclusion that in many cases abnormalities of character contributed to the development of homosexuality. His views on these matters have not gained universal acceptance, and to some extent they run counter to the observation, repeatedly stressed in this book, that homosexuals as a whole cannot be said to belong to any particular character type. However, the Freudian theories deserve most careful consideration, for they do give insight into certain neurotic symptoms that otherwise appear meaningless, and they also help to explain the frequency of homosexual tendencies in certain types of mentally abnormal persons. At the same time one must constantly beware of the 'fallacy of the undistributed middle'. Because homosexual developments often occur in connexion with certain abnormalities, it in no way follows that the majority of homosexuals suffer from these abnormalities.

On these questions Freud expressed himself cautiously, much more cautiously than some later exponents of psycho-analysis. He was well aware that 'In men the most complete mental masculinity can be combined with inversion', and he rejected Ulrich's facile explanation of 'a feminine brain in a masculine body'. He emphasized that 'Psycho-analytic research is most decidedly opposed to any attempt at separating off homosexuals from the rest of mankind as a group of a special character.' However, in describing their early development, he advanced the theory that, following a short-lived fixation to mother, male homosexuals tend to identify *themselves* as a woman. Just as the woman with the musical father tried to resolve her fixation by herself becoming like him, so the mother-fixated man tries to identify with mother and himself assume the mother's role. He then sets out to look for a young man he can love as his mother loved him, or at any rate as he would have liked his mother to love him. The object of his choice, therefore, is really his own image, and in a sense he might be said to be in love with himself. This Freud called *narcissism*, from the Greek legend of Narcissus, the young man who fell in love with his own reflection [63]. According to the Freudians, both narcissism and Oedipal guilt feature in the genesis of homosexuality.

Arrest of sexual development at the narcissistic stage, in addition to showing itself in sexual perversion, is supposed to produce a vain, self-glorifying personality. The typical 'narcissistic character' delights in the devotion of others, but gives little warmth in return. The 'narcissistic type' of homosexual takes enormous pride in his appearance and may go in for body-building exercises. In personal relationships, however, he tends to be cold and self-centred. Having captured the affections of some youth, he is quite likely to refuse him sexual favours on the grounds that 'sex is weakening'.

Some analysts believe that infanto-homosexuals, those who lust after children, are mainly narcissistic types. The image of 'mother's little boy' remains planted in their unconscious, so that even in adult life they continue to chase after children.

It seems open to doubt whether the concept of narcissism applies to the majority of homosexuals. In some cases the first stage, the process of identification with womanhood, shows very obviously. The boy who plays with dolls and likes to dress as a girl may grow up into a 'pansy' who adores perfume, make-up, and all the trappings of femininity. But such effeminate men do not always show narcissistic character traits, nor do they always seek youths; some of them definitely prefer an older man as a pseudo-'husband'. Although some observers believe that narcissistic character traits such as vanity, self-display, and shallowness in personal relationships appear very often among homosexuals, this has never been properly established. Superficially, the behaviour of certain city coteries conforms to this pattern, but such coteries comprise only a small minority of homosexuals, and even in their case their outlook is probably influenced more by social circumstances than by deep-rooted narcissism. In any event, the very same traits appear all too often in heterosexuals.

In the matter of infanto-homosexuality, emotional arrest at the narcissistic stage of childhood may in part account for an attraction to young boys, for this type of sexual abnormality is linked more closely with immature personalities; but other influences are equally important. Some men, though emotionally orientated to homosexuality, resist the commission of overt acts on account of fear, disgust, or moral disapproval. They stay continent and so never learn to relate sexual thoughts to adults. Their only acquaintance with actual sexual practices is the memory of schoolboy play. If at some time or other their sexual drive finally overcomes their resistance, their first impulse is to return to the only type of pleasure they have known, so they seek out a child in preference to an adult. In contrast, the man who makes little attempt to resist his homosexual inclinations, and so has continuous experience with persons of his own age from adolescence onwards, has no reason to turn to children for gratification.

2. ANAL FIXATION

One aspect of psycho-analytic theory not so far mentioned, but very relevant to the question of homosexual practices, concerns the mode of development of erotic sensibilities. According to the analysts, when the sexual drive begins to manifest in infancy, the impulses are at first comparatively diffuse. Only by a long process of narrowing down and elimination does the aim of genital union with a person of the opposite sex assume predominance. Before reaching that final stage the child passes through various phases in which general bodily stimulation, sucking and the like, afford as much pleasure as manipulation of the genitals. In other words, the sexual drive is at first undifferentiated, both as regards the indiscriminate choice of a male or female love object and also as regards the body zones from which physical satisfaction is derived. In the mature adult copulation is the essential sexual activity, but even then sexual arousal often involves stimulation of other body zones, as is shown by the fondling, kissing, and biting that take place in normal love play. Freud believed that children go through several definable stages before the genitals become the prime source of erotic delight. First the *oral* stage, when mouth contacts and sucking give satisfaction. Then comes the *anal* stage, when the child derives pleasure from the buttock area and from bowel movements. Lastly comes the stage of *genital* primacy.

Since, in our culture, kissing does not qualify as a perversion, oral contacts remain a subsidiary form of sexual pleasure with normal adults. Anal practices, however, come under the strictest taboo. The thought of sodomy or the like seems to many persons exquisitely horrible, for we are brought up to regard lavatories, the bowel excrement, and all their associations as unclean and revolting. The way dogs sniff at the bowel and show interest in excreta seems quite horrible; but, were it not for artificially acquired disgust, we ourselves might show traces of this animal behaviour. As it is, some children have to be weaned of the habit of handling and smearing excreta, and lunatics who have lost their repressions and regressed to infantile behaviour display an unabashed interest in dirt. Even in the sane, the sexual drive often overcomes the acquired disgust, and many persons in our culture, and many more in other cultures, make use of the erotic potentialities of the anal zone in the practice of sodomy. Extreme disgust at the sight and smell of excrement reflects an early acquired emotional reaction against anything anal. Admittedly faeces carry germs, but the disgust scarcely proceeds from reasoned considerations and it is not an inborn instinct. In its way it is as irrational as the attitude of the hysterical girl who expresses disgust with normal sex because the male organ passes urine. Freud claimed that, during the anal stage of development, before they have fully acquired the sense of disgust, normal infants display a fairly obvious pleasure in bowel movements. Some children delight to hold back their stools so that finally they can enjoy the maximum stimulation. For this reason they are apt to spend an unnecessarily long time on the chamber pot and can only be persuaded with difficulty to evacuate their bowel [64].

Apart from perverts who never relinquish the pleasures of the anal zone, Freud recognized a class of adults in whom anal sexuality is still active, although repressed and manifest only in disguised form. The psycho-analysis of certain abnormal personality types, namely those characterized by a combination of obsessive orderliness, parsimony, and obstinacy, led him to conclude that such persons are influenced by strong, repressed anal interests. The obstinacy and pleasure in hoarding he interpreted as adult relics of the infantile habit of obstinately hoarding faeces. Their neatness, orderliness, and excessive cleanliness he interpreted as reactions against repressed desires to do the exact opposite – to play with dirt. This connexion between miserly characteristics and unconscious love of 'dirt' had long been apparent in such everyday expressions as 'filthy lucre', 'making his pile', 'the goose that lays the golden eggs', and (in German) *'Dukatenscheisser'*. Psycho-analysis of these so-called anal characters confirms that their inner fantasy life tends to be preoccupied with bowel functions and associated matters [65].

Since many homosexuals take to sodomy, the question arises whether, as a group, they display the character traits attributed by Freud to persons with strong anal interests. So far as I know the matter has never been adequately investigated, but there is a widespread impression that a certain type of homosexual does run true to form. Men who prefer the active role in sodomy (i.e., those for whom sodomy

a substitute for normal copulation), and men to whom
e sex role is a matter of indifference provided that pleasure
mutual, do not come into the category; but men who
tain pleasure solely from passive sodomy tend to show
me typically 'anal' traits. They fuss over dress and toilet,
te to soil their hands, keep their things meticulously neat
d tidy, and live to a strict, conventional routine. But one
nnot set too much store by this observation. Homosexuals
10 practise sodomy are not all anally fixated in the Freud-
1 sense, which implies an emotional blockage resulting in
rest of development at the anal stage and failure to adjust
genital sexuality. Since they cannot have normal inter-
urse, homosexuals are prone to experiment with extra-
nital erotic zones, and many take to sodomy simply
·cause they discover it provides a mechanically convenient
·rm of sexual gratification. The man who takes part in
domy need be no more 'anal fixated' than the man who
sses his girl friend is necessarily fixated at the 'oral stage'
development. Moreover, as has already been emphasized,
·domy is not an exclusively homosexual phenomenon, and
·nal characters' need not be in the least homosexually
.clined. In fact, most persons classified by analysts as anal
·naracter-neurotics come for treatment on account of their
·ascible, difficult temperaments, and not because of any
·bvious homosexual problem. Similarly, the narcissistic
·pes often seek help because their immature emotional
·utlook prevents their settling down to stable marital rela-
·ons. The connexion between homosexuality and anal and
·arcissistic fixations is, to say the least, tenuous. While these
·xations may be important in some cases, it seems a fair
·onclusion that they have no direct connexion with homo-
·exuality in general.

INSANE DELUSIONS

·ccording to psycho-analysts, exclusive homosexuality is
·onnected with other abnormalities both in the way it begins
·nd in the possible consequences once it has developed. Thus
·hey claim that narcissistic and anal fixations may bring

about a homosexual orientation, and that in turn homo
sexual orientation may sometimes precipitate insanity. I
Freudian theory, the familiar mental derangement 'persecu
tion mania', technically called paranoia, arises from conflic
over homosexual tendencies. In this form of insanity th
sufferer imagines himself the victim of wicked plots an
scheming enemies. His delusional system of ideas frequentl
centres upon one particular person who becomes in th
paranoiac's mind an arch-fiend with diabolical powers. I
typical cases he complains of sexual tortures in the form o
horrible sensations or disgusting thoughts, which, he say
his enemy inflicts upon him from a distance by means o
'rays', 'hypnotism', or 'telepathy'.

Superficially such delusions appear nonsensical, but Freu
showed that they have a thinly disguised homosexua
flavour. The supposed enemy is really someone for who
the insane person experiences sexual feeling, but a violen
reaction against the guilty attraction causes him to fly t
the opposite extreme and assert that the offending individua
is an object of hate and not of love. Hence the delusion take
the form of a denial, a protest that 'he interferes with m
but I don't like it, I hate him'. In other words this type o
delusional insanity consists of an extreme instance of over
compensation for repressed homosexual feelings [20].

Freud demonstrated this mechanism in detail in the cas
of Dr Schreber, a Dresden judge. This man fell a prey to
mixture of grandiose and persecutory delusions, and pub
lished a mad account of his ideas in a book entitled *Memoir
of a Neurotic*. In a lengthy paper Freud examined the lon
published account of Dr Schreber's delusions, and showe
the unmistakable homosexual significance of much of th
material [66].

Dr Schreber fell ill in October 1893, suffering from hypo
chondriacal fears and ideas of persecution. He believed tha
horrible things were happening to his body, that it wa
diseased and decomposing, and that in addition his sexua
parts were being handled and misused in revolting way
Tormenting voices told him he was being turned into

oman. He would sit motionless for hours, completely pre-
cupied with these hallucinatory impressions. He hated
hat was happening to him so much that he tried to kill
mself. Gradually the disturbance became less acute. After
ne years Dr Schreber was able to pay attention to the
atside world and deal with practical affairs. He secured his
lease from hospital, but he still adhered to an elaborate
stem of delusory ideas and felt impelled to write his
emoirs.

In the earlier stages of his illness Dr Schreber believed he
as being emasculated for the purpose of sexual abuse, and
at the perpetrator of the outrage was his physician, Pro-
ssor Fleisig. Later his delusion changed in character and
e came to accept, even to welcome the idea of conversion
to a woman, believing this miracle to be a preliminary to
e still greater, namely his assumption of the role of
ligious Redeemer of the world. He came to believe that
od himself, and not Professor Fleisig, was the prime
stigator of his persecutions, and that he was being prepared
r a voluptuous union with God. He felt he must abandon
s former principles of restraint and sexual continence, and
cknowledge his duty to assume the role of God's Wife and
e world's Redeemer. The bulk of his book consisted of
ccounts of numerous secondary delusions and elaborations
l stemming from this central theme.

Freud noted that Dr Schreber's illness commenced with a
ervous collapse' while his wife was away on holiday. One
ight during her absence he experienced several emissions
f semen. When she returned he no longer felt he wanted
er. At about the same period, he reported that, while in a
ate between sleeping and waking, the idea came to him
at it would be nice to be a woman and submit to copula-
on. All this fits in with Freud's interpretation that the
chreber fantasy was a reaction against homosexual desires.
t first even the delusions about the abominable Fleisig
roved inadequate to salve Schreber's conscience, and he
ied to kill himself. Only after he had developed the in-
enious delusion about submitting to God, and could indulge

in feminine sexual fantasies with a clear conscience, was tl
conflict sufficiently solved to enable him to make a parti
recovery. Once he had achieved a state of 'peaceful c
existence' with his delusions, he ceased to be a suicidal ris

Freud certainly put paranoia in a new light, and no o1
today denies that paranoid delusions frequently reve
blatant homosexual conflicts. Sometimes the homosexu
trends are apparent in the patient's behaviour, and tl
conflict is fully conscious [91, 166]. But it is not general
accepted that homosexual conflict is the chief feature in a
cases of paranoia [114, 188]. D. Henderson and R. D. Gi
lespie in their *Textbook of Psychiatry* point out that reactio
against forbidden heterosexual desires may also form tl
background of paranoid delusions. One must also bear i
mind that the discovery of the psychological meaning of tl
delusions does not fully explain the cause of the illness an
does not help to cure it. Paranoiacs will not respond to reasc
or to psychological explanations; they have their own fixe
ideas and no one can change them. Only a small minorit
of those with homosexual conflicts react by developin
paranoia, so the mere existence of such a conflict cann
fully account for a delusional reaction.

Many psychiatrists do not consider paranoia a disease i
its own right, but look upon it as just one form of schiz
phrenia. Originally paranoia was distinguished fro1
schizophrenia because paranoiac patients have delusions bi
do not display the hallucinations, disturbances of thougl
processes, and general deterioration of personality so con
mon in schizophrenia. In practice, if paranoiacs are followe
up long enough, other symptoms besides delusions usuall
appear, and gradually the picture assumes a more typic2
schizophrenic form. The importance of this lies in i1
implications regarding the causation of the disorder. Ther
is known to be a big inherited, constitutional element in th
tendency to schizophrenic reactions. Recent research als
suggests that schizophrenic symptoms may be a sign of a1
underlying physical disorder, perhaps a poisoning of th
system due to a failure in the chemical processes connecte

ith the hormone adrenalin. In any event, the whole
uestion of the causation of schizophrenia, which is the
ommonest and most serious form of insanity, involves much
nore than just homosexual conflict. Nevertheless, homo-
exual conflict does come into the picture in many cases of
chizophrenia, and not just in paranoia. Psychiatrists have
requently commented on the prevalence of homosexual
rends among schizophrenics [150], and the Rorschach and
ther personality tests, applied to schizophrenic patients,
ave confirmed the existence of an apparent association
etween the two conditions [21, 33, 167, 202].

A. J. Rosanoff [164] puts forward the view that chaotic
exuality (i.e., unsuitably directed sexual drives) forms the
asis of all schizophrenia. He believes that homosexuality
nd other perverse inclinations do not in themselves cause
nental disorder, but that when the individual makes de-
ermined efforts to control such tendencies by repressing
hem the acute mental conflict which results makes break-
lown almost inevitable. If repression allows the chaotic
exual drive no outlet, then the sexual impulses force their
vay through in disguised form and gain symbolic expression
n delusions and hallucinatory projections. Rosanoff inter-
orets many of the characteristic symptoms of schizophrenia,
uch as aggressive paranoid outbursts, persecutory delusions,
nd feelings of being 'influenced' bodily or mentally, as
lefence mechanisms against homosexual feelings. His theory
ccounts for the observation that schizophrenic men and
vomen, given the Terman and Miles masculinity-femininity
questionnaire (see page 43), rate significantly towards the
verage score for the opposite sex [24].

. LATENT HOMOSEXUALITY, ALCOHOLISM,
    AND CRIME

Although insane delusions are foreign to ordinary experi-
nce and somewhat horrible to contemplate, they have been
lealt with at some length because they provide clear ex-
imples of an important mental process that occurs in
ubtler form in many persons who are far from insane.

Apart from insane delusions, A. J. Rosanoff believed that violent reactions against homosexual tendencies could also lead to neurosis, to suicidal tendencies, to an escape into alcoholism or drug addiction, and to strange forms of criminal behaviour [164]. Psycho-analysts often find that the man with an extremely emotional attitude to homosexuality, one who advocates 'the gas chamber for those vermin', is really in this way compensating for his own latent homosexual tendencies. There are none so eager to root out perversion as those who themselves feel insecure against temptation. But the reaction does not always take so militant a form. Pressure from repressed homosexual inclinations often produces acute or chronic anxiety neurosis. Analysts report that anxiety states, palpitations, sweats, phobias, and the like frequently turn out to be caused by unconscious homosexual tendencies which, when they threaten to break forth into full consciousness, produce feelings of acute fear or tension. Some latent homosexuals, if placed in a situation of intolerable temptation, break out into a feverish panic amounting almost to temporary manic insanity. This condition, called 'homosexual panic' or Kempf's Disease, is an entity well recognized in some of the American textbooks on psychiatry [103].

Psychiatrists have long recognized flight into alcoholism as one way in which latent homosexuals seek escape from their conflicts [150, 174]. The sense of well-being and the loss of tension and self-consciousness produced by alcohol come as a great boon to the conflict-ridden. Moreover, drinking enables men to enjoy intimate male companionship without provoking comment, and so affords a particularly attractive outlet for the latent homosexual. Alcohol damps down inhibitions, and some of those who would scorn the thought when sober will indulge in deviant sexual practices when drunk. It also aids forgetfulness. Some men, when their tensions reach an unbearable pitch, rush away on a mad 'binge', during which they have homosexual adventures, afterwards returning to their ordinary life untroubled by any conscious recollection of their lapse. The American novel, *The Lost Week End,* by Charles Jackson, deals with such a case.[1] In addition it has been noted that alcoholics make unreasonably suspicious and jealous husbands, although they may be virtually impotent, and this has been advanced as an argument in favour of a homosexual component, the jealousy being interpreted as a projection on to the wife of the husband's own desire to be unfaithful with men. Perhaps this explanation applies to some cases, but the fact must be taken into account that alcoholic poisoning itself may decrease potency, and this is turn may give rise to jealous fears, quite apart from any homosexual problem.

It is now widely accepted that homosexuals may be useful, productive people and not in the least anti-social aside from their sexual peculiarity [32, 189]. Nevertheless, there is supposed to be a connexion between homosexuality and the 'degenerate', criminal trends found in psychopathic types. 'Psychopathic personalities' have no particular defect of intelligence; they are neither inhibited by conflicts, like neurotics, nor withdrawn into a fantasy world, like the insane, but all the same they cannot fit into society. They are the born drifters – shiftless, anti-social characters who distrust everyone and everything, and would rather lie and thieve than knuckle down to a steady job. All their lives they remain aggressive, sullen 'problem children'. They are said to be prone to homosexuality and other perversions, but they show none of the deep-seated guilt and remorse of the neurotic who tries to repress his inclinations. Psychopaths are the last people to try to battle against their instincts; they just obey first impulses regardless of social codes. Being incapable of prolonged or deep personal attachments, they seek only an immediate outlet for their lust. Often they find it less troublesome to satisfy themselves with another man than to woo a woman or pay a prostitute. The life histories of psychopaths show that usually they come from disorganized or broken homes, and that many have been in and out of institutions all their lives. In addition to constitutional

1. The bowdlerized film version of this story contains no reference to the essential theme.

factors (revealed in some cases by abnormal brain rhythms)
it appears that their root trouble is early deprivation of love
and the absence of stable parental figures. This is reflected
in their restless, drifting lives and distrustful anti-social
attitudes as well as in their sexuality, which remains im
mature and unstable in its direction. They lack the control
ling influences required to channel the sexual drive into
exclusive homosexuality or exclusive heterosexuality. The
psychopath never identifies himself with any consistent code
of behaviour, save perhaps that of the rebel, and so tends to
remain a disgruntled bisexual.

This brief survey of psychiatric observations shows that
conflict over homosexuality may enter into the genesis of all
kinds of mental disorders, from drug addiction and anxiety
neurosis to delusional insanity. This is not altogether sur
prising, for latent homosexuality is such an exceedingly
common source of conflict that one might expect to find it
responsible for precipitating many breakdowns. Some theorists, however, go further, and assert that particular
abnormalities, such as alcoholism and paranoia, are merely
disguised forms of homosexuality. Such views seem a little
exaggerated. It is probable that homosexual conflict bears
no direct relation to any particular mental illness but simply
provokes breakdowns of one sort or another by setting up
unbearable tensions. The form the breakdown takes will
depend upon the individual personality. The rigid, uncompromising character who cannot bear the least slur on his
own grandiose self-evaluation will tend to develop paranoia;
the weak-willed, self-pitying type who looks for an easy way
out will more likely take to alcohol; the worrying, introspective individual will develop anxiety neurosis. All these
disorders have this in common: they are associated with
futile attempts to repress disagreeable tendencies. Overt
homosexuals who fully admit their own abnormality may
experience twinges of conscience and suffer from rejection
by their fellows, but they rarely succumb to the complete
mental collapse that comes from the ravages of internal
strife.

Latent homosexual tendencies are too common to provide a complete explanation of mental illness, although the concept has proved invaluable to an understanding of mental symptoms. Just as in the case of illnesses based on the equally ubiquitous Oedipal conflict, one needs to discover why, in certain individuals, the conflict rages with such unusual violence. The root causes are no doubt substantially the same as those which make for homosexuality in general (mother fixation, etc.), but with the difference that latent homosexuals resist with peculiar vigour any yielding to aberrant impulses. In cases like that of the alcoholic, who goes off every now and then on a homosexual spree, repression is not very deep and the impulses come constantly very close to overt expression. In other cases, the unconscious homosexual fantasies exist only in the form of deeply repressed relics of infantile feelings. Though they may indirectly give rise to neurotic symptoms, they are no more likely to gain expression in overt acts than the unconscious incest-fantasies of the Oedipal stage of infancy. Between these two extremes of almost open perversion and of fantasies so deeply repressed that their presence can only be revealed by prolonged psycho-analytic probing, lie the majority of cases of homosexual neurosis.

Following upon this discussion of the homosexual factors often found in cases of mental illness, the previous assertion that the direction taken by the sexual urge has little relation to abnormal mental traits needs some qualification. The statement is true of the majority of persons who resolve their conflicts one way or another, either by developing heterosexuality or by fully and openly accepting their homosexual inclinations. On the other hand, those who remain in the dangerously unstable condition of partially repressed homosexuality are liable to develop all manner of disorders.

10

Treatment for the Individual

GIVEN a simple choice, no one in his right mind would choose to be homosexual. However strongly they protest their freedom from conventional morality, sexual deviants cannot escape a lurking guilt. The fact that many decent folk regard them as moral lepers renders them furtive and unsure, or else forces them into flaunting bravado. Though they wear no visible crutches, their disability is real enough. The large number of otherwise respectable men arrested for loitering in public lavatories gives some indication of the depths of frustration to which many sink. Paradoxically, they long for social acceptance, but cannot bear the thought of change. Heterosexual life has no meaning for confirmed homosexuals, for their emotions are so fixed that neither social pressure nor calculated self-interest will shift them.

Homosexuals vary enormously, both in themselves and in the circumstances in which they come to the attention of a doctor; but for many of them there is but little hope of effecting a radical change. Dr Desmond Curran, a psychiatrist who served on the Wolfenden Committee, states that the chances of cure in confirmed cases are negligible and that the psychiatrist should concentrate on making the patient a better-adjusted homosexual and not aspire to convert him to heterosexuality [38]. Referring to the case of an intelligent man of thirty-nine who had practised homosexuality since adolescence without obvious guilt, and then sought advice as to whether he was curable, Dr Curran states: 'The only answer that could be given to such a patient was that the prospect of this would be small, and that whether he indulged in homosexual acts or not was something that he must decide for himself' [37]. In a study of 100 cases seen in private practice, Curran and Parr [39]

eport that 25 patients treated psychotherapeutically re-
eived no apparent benefit in terms of changed sexual
preference of behaviour as compared with 25 matched
patients not so treated. Some clinicians hold contrary views,
n particular Clifford Allen in this country [3] and Albert
Ellis in the United States. The latter maintains that homosexuals who really want to change, but who are held back by
irrational fears of intercourse with women, can be helped.
Describing the results of psychotherapy (from 5 to 220
essions per patient) on 28 men with severe homosexual
problems he reports that 18 improved in terms of heterosexual adjustment [50]. He gives no Kinsey ratings, so perhaps few of his cases were of the confirmed, exclusive type
that other therapists find unchangeable. A spontaneous
drift towards heterosexuality as age increases is suggested
by Kinsey's figures, and may occur without treatment.

Some authorities, especially those who believe the condition arises from an inborn, inalterable disposition, bluntly
refuse to allow that psychotherapy has any application.

Thus Dr Stanley-Jones writes:

There can be no question of asking the invert to accept the
ordinary standards of heterosexual morality, and any course of
therapy which seeks to reverse the fundamental pattern is not
only fore-doomed to failure, as all the reported cases testify, but
is also quite indefensible when regarded in the light of absolute
morality: attempted 'treatment' or alteration of the basic personality of an inborn homosexual can only be described as a
moral outrage. [178].

The treatment of homosexuals is still an unsettled question among psycho-analysts [179]. Some of them make
unduly optimistic claims about the possibility of cure, but
Freud himself held out little hope. He noted that the homosexual is usually unable to give up the object of his love, and
that therapeutic successes are few. 'If he comes to be treated
at all, it is mostly through the pressure of external motives,
such as the social disadvantages and dangers attaching to
his choice of object ...' Sometimes he secretly hopes for
treatment to fail so as 'to obtain from the striking failure of

his attempt the feeling of satisfaction that he has done everything possible against his abnormality, to which he can now resign himself with an easy conscience' [67].

Freud's contention that homosexuals rarely seek treatment, except when driven by loneliness or fear, has had ample confirmation in the experience of later observers [149].

Although psycho-analysts appear to regard homosexuality as theoretically amenable to treatment, some of them recognize a class of 'incurables' whom they classify as 'constitutional', and nearly all of them admit that many cases are exceedingly tough nuts to crack. They claim that sexual deviants become so set in their habits, and derive so much pleasure from their practices, that they lack incentive to change. Be this as it may, the plain fact of the matter is that in well-established cases prolonged psychological treatment offers only a slender hope of change.

Other forms of treatment offer no hope at all and hardly deserve consideration. One gets the impression that at one time or another diverse methods have been tried more for the sake of doing something than on any reasoned plan. Why, for instance, should electro-convulsant therapy, because it helps to clear melancholia, be expected to change homosexuals? Its application to homosexuals has rightly fallen into disrepute [187]. One authority claimed to cure homosexuality and lesbianism with the convulsant drug metrazol, and reported six cases to prove the point, but the idea appears to have died a natural death [153]. Androgenic hormones increase desire in homosexual males without changing their nature. Oestrogens have some practical value, in that they reduce sexual appetite in men, but they in no sense effect a cure, and may not even relieve guilt feelings. Persons who imagine themselves unnatural monsters will not necessarily cease to feel that way merely because their impulses become somewhat less compulsive; indeed, the knowledge that they have been chemically castrated may add to their sense of shame.

As a means of curing neurotic complexes, hypnotism went out of fashion when psycho-analysis gained the ascendancy.

Once it became feasible to deal directly with the emotional confusions that were the root of the trouble, psychiatrists came to regard the temporary relief of symptoms by force of suggestion as a definitely inferior method of treatment. Removal of a twitch or other symptom by means of hypnotic suggestion does not cure the underlying nervousness, which may find expression in other and worse ways, and as the underlying inhibitions in established cases of sexual deviation seem to be very deep-rooted and intractable, one would not expect hypnotic suggestion to do much good. Imperative commands to cohabit with a woman might simply increase the patient's conflicts, or even precipitate an acute mental breakdown. Nevertheless, in the older German literature on perversions, hypnotism is featured as a powerful therapeutic weapon. Baron von Schrenck-Notzing regarded the establishment of sexual intercourse as the principal requirement for cure, and published details of various cases in which he and other doctors had succeeded in this purpose with the aid of hypnotic suggestion [169]. His approach strikes the modern reader as crude. He concentrates simply on encouraging copulation, on the assumption that actual practice will overcome inhibitions and stimulate normal desire. Some of the pathetic letters from patients describing their attempts to fulfil the hypnotic suggestions testify to the limitations of this treatment. If a man overcomes his impotence with women through achieving preliminary tumescence by dint of masturbation to the accompaniment of homosexual fantasies, this counts as a considerable success. Nevertheless, it seems evident from the case reports that some previously impotent men do in fact succeed in performing the act of copulation and even acquire some heterosexual desire as a result of hypnotic suggestions; but there is a definite tendency to relapse, which is understandable considering that it is the physician's commands and not the patient's own free choice that dictate the excursions into heterosexual practice. The success of the treatment in certain cases shows that the accomplishment of satisfactory intercourse will sometimes overcome the inhibitions regarding heterosexuality; but the

advisability of using undue pressure, by hypnotism or otherwise, to force copulation is open to question. In all probability the few who did well under hypnotism were those with
only mild or superficial inhibitions, and given encouragement by their doctor they might have achieved the same
result of their own volition. It is not clear whether the ones
who failed to respond suffered any ill effects. Hypnotism is
still used sometimes in the treatment of homosexuals, but
as an adjunct to psycho-analysis rather than as a means of
forcing copulation [168].

The various deterrents that have at one time or another
been applied – imprisonment, ostracism, torture, and execution have been no more effective than when similar measures
were taken against fornication. They may succeed in en-
forcing continence, but do nothing to change homosexual
potentialities. In addition, they are apt to provoke worse
disorders than the condition they were meant to improve.
Much the same considerations apply to the different forms
of financial coercion, threats, and 'brain washing' to which
well-meaning families sometimes subject their homosexual
offspring. Abuse and lamentations from his family increase
the homosexual's problems, but do nothing to help him
towards a solution. Religious exhortation, which places
emphasis on the wickedness of yielding to impulse, encourages continence by building up inhibitions based on guilt
feeling. If the result were a calm, deliberate decision to
behave chastely it would not be unhealthy, but injudiciously
expressed religious precepts tend to exaggerate the sufferer's
sense of guilt and shame. Instead of inducing strong-minded
self-control, this leads to great misery and to desperate
attempts to deny the very existence of the offending impulses. The repressions and mental conflicts so provoked
may turn the individual into a worse social nuisance and
misfit than he would have been if he had simply stayed
homosexual. One cannot blame the priest for this regret-
table outcome. It is all very well for a psychiatrist like Dr
Desmond Curran to detach himself from moral questions
and tell the patient, 'Decide for yourself', but the priest has

to teach a set code which includes the rule that homosexual acts are wicked and inexcusable.

Treatment through imprisonment is a contradiction in terms. Those who try to justify prison sentences for homosexuality on the grounds that loss of liberty provides impetus for conversion to heterosexuality are ignorant of the elementary facts of the matter. The argument that punishment acts as a deterrent to potential offenders provides the only rational basis for imprisonment. But for the individual who is incarcerated, segregation in an over-crowded gaol serves only to encourage his homosexual practices (see pages 73-4). This is not to decry the good work of some of the prison therapists, who do much to help the homosexuals in their charge, but prospects of radical cure are greatly reduced by a prison atmosphere [132]. The only hope of changing sexual orientation lies in the removing of inhibitions by means of psychological treatment accompanied by a step-by-step adjustment to heterosexual life. A man submerged in the living death of prison routine, and cut off from all feminine company, is under the worst possible conditions for receiving treatment. As Dr Stanley-Jones has said, imprisonment 'is as futile from the point of view of treatment as to hope to rehabilitate a chronic alcoholic by giving him occupational therapy in a brewery' [179]. In effect, the circumstances of prison life, and the limited amount of time prison psychiatrists can give to the matter, virtually preclude all hope of radical cures. The most that can be done in prisons under existing circumstances is on the lines described by Dr J. C. Mackwood, one-time psychotherapist at Wormwood Scrubs. This institution provided a separate ward for prisoners undergoing treatment. There they met together as a group and talked out their problems under the doctor's guidance. This group treatment had a remedial and educational effect on neurotic prisoners. Dr Mackwood remarked that sometimes the group contained over 50 per cent of homosexuals. He aimed to help them by discussion of their disturbed relations with other people, but he admitted the task could have been done under more suitable conditions.

In fact, he advocated legal reform that would not make socially harmless behaviour a crime [131].

In considering the question of therapy in prisons, one must take account of the fact that many of the men who find their way to gaol are not the sort to benefit from psychological treatment under any circumstances. Dr F. J. Taylor, in a survey of 96 cases sent to Brixton Prison for homosexual offences in 1946, found only one that was suitable for psychotherapy and had good prospects. The 96 men comprised 66 who were classified as pseudo-homosexuals because they were thought to have indulged only as a substitute for normal sexual relations, 5 who were prostitutes, 12 who were bisexuals and capable of full satisfaction with either sex, and only 13 who were complete homosexuals. Of these 13, 7 were in prison in spite of previous psychotherapy and 3 emphatically refused to have treatment [183].

The best hope of radical change in long-standing cases lies in psycho-analysis. Most people nowadays are familiar with the broad outline of the technique, which consists of long and repeated sessions of talking out inner thoughts and fantasies. The neurotic sufferer has a sort of compulsion to dwell upon topics related to his conflicts, but he tends always to skirt round the edge without ever coming to grips with the real issues. The analyst directs his attention to the focal points of his disturbance, forces him to verbalize ever more fully and frankly his conflicting emotions and fantasies, and by this means guides him along the difficult path of self-revelation. In the process, old conflicts flare up, and the patient relives with dramatic intensity the turbulent emotions of his formative years. For him analysis is a painful struggle. His neurotic symptoms or sexual aberrations represent a comfortable, half-way adjustment to life. He wants to grow out of this half-way stage, but at the same time he clings grimly to his neurotic refuge. Treatment, therefore, consists of a protracted battle between fears and resistance to change on the one hand and desire for normality on the other. But the process of changing the deeply ingrained emotional habits of a lifetime cannot be hurried.

Full psycho-analysis may mean five hour-long sessions every week for a period of years. Even so, for many patients the task proves too difficult, and they slip back into their neurotic ways. Psycho-analysis is successful only in carefully selected cases. It is a lengthy, costly, and exacting business which demands of the patient a certain intelligence, a capacity for self-scrutiny, and a sincere desire to go through anything for the sake of a cure.

The analyst's technique is essentially the same whether the patient presents obvious neurotic symptoms or whether the only complaint concerns abnormal sexual inclinations. Persons in a tense state, with prominent anxiety symptoms and guilt feelings (as in the case of the man with the pregnancy phobia), are easy to help because their conflicts are close to the surface and their miserable condition provides a strong motive for change. The difficult cases are those who have long since accepted homosexual practices as a part of the natural order of things and have no pressing motive for trying to unearth their past conflicts. In all cases the analyst directs attention to the inhibitions that prevent heterosexual development. He is under no compulsion to explain how it is that the patient can love a person of his own sex. To the analyst such love is neither unnatural nor incomprehensible, but simply immature. When the barriers of unconscious fear and guilt are removed the patient is free to choose himself a more appropriate love object.

Unfortunately, in many cases the discovery of infantile fears of incestuous relationships and suchlike fantasies, which the analysts believe to have been the original cause of the turning away from normal sex, does not in itself bring about a disappearance of homosexual desires. When homosexual reactions have been firmly conditioned by experience over a period of years, they are exceedingly difficult to change; and although the presence of tension and guilt is a hopeful sign, it does not guarantee a cure. Notwithstanding much unhappiness and self-blame, and despite considerable insight into the psychological quirks that first set them on the road to homosexuality, many remain unable to change

their outlook. A symptom with a purely protective function
readily disappears once it has outworn its usefulness. To
give a crude example, a girl who has hysterical fainting
attacks whenever she feels threatened by a sexual approach
ceases to faint once she has understood and overcome her
fears. But homosexuality, though it may arise as a neurotic
protection against heterosexual temptation, can become an
end in itself. Consequently, the homosexual may resist conversion long after the original basis of his flight from the
opposite sex has been laid bare. He may prefer his way of
life because he has grown up with it and become thoroughly
adjusted to it. The fact that a man resists change does not
always mean he is weak-willed or obstinate. Shallow, un-
principled characters are content to find sex wherever the
opportunity presents, but the mature homosexual has adjusted his loves and his loyalties to a particular style of life.
As has been remarked earlier, it is as difficult to eradicate
the emotional and sensual inclinations of a developed
homosexual as it would be to quell the natural desires of a
normal adult. But one must not lose sight of the fact that
outstanding successes have been claimed. In one published
case a man of forty, who liked the passive role in sodomy
and had practised homosexuality for 32 years, was cured in
the course of 85 sessions over a period of eight months
[157].

All that has just been said on the side of pessimism applies
only to fully developed cases. Curran emphasized that it is
unsafe to diagnose a state of established homosexuality before the age of twenty-five. Perhaps he carries the principle
too far, but undoubtedly many young men who practise
homosexuality in their late teens or early twenties grow out
of the habit after meeting a suitable woman and settling
down to heterosexual life. These are not true homosexuals
harbouring deep-rooted and intractable inhibitions with
regard to the opposite sex; they are simply late starters in
heterosexuality. In Western culture a youth arrives at
physiological maturity long before mature expression of his
sexual impulses becomes permissible or practicable. At the

me when their impulses first assume adult intensity, most
dolescent males are still engrossed in school activities,
ports, work-training, and similar masculine pursuits. As a
onsequence their first sexual essays are so often with their
wn sex that a homosexual phase, characterized by undis-
riminating pruriency and emotional fixations of the hero-
vorshipping type, is widely regarded as a normal feature of
dolescence. Some young persons take a long time to work
hrough this phase, not because they have a fixed homo-
exual orientation, but because their way of life leaves no
oom for the opposite sex, so that the full impact of hetero-
exual influences is delayed. Occasionally relatives seek
sychiatric advice on behalf of some young person with an
dolescent 'crush' on a friend. In most cases they can safely
e reassured. Provided the young person shows no tendency
o adopt manners and habits more appropriate to a member
f the opposite sex, and provided he has no special aversion
o mixed company, then permanent sexual deviation need
ot be anticipated. Given the right encouragement and
pportunity for easy social contacts with the opposite sex, the
ealthy adolescent soon develops heterosexual interests in
pite of early homosexual enthusiasms [16, 160].

Even if a man reaches the early twenties without ever
eeking out a woman, it should not be assumed that his
exual inclinations are completely inverted without first
arefully investigating his attitude and circumstances. Age
s not the only consideration. A man or woman with no
ractical experience of sex save an occasional homosexual
dventure, followed by guilt and remorse, has more chance
f developing heterosexuality than a younger person who
has regularly indulged in deviant practices for several years.
A man who only practises homosexuality *faute de mieux,*
ecause social backwardness or fear of responsibility prevents him making advances to the women he wants, has a
better prospect of cure than another with youth on his side
but with no interest in women. When homosexual behaviour
represents a precarious solution of current conflicts, or reflects the pressure of external circumstances, a change may

well come about. When it arises from deep emotional prejudices against normal sexual contacts, reinforced by long
experience and acceptance of a homosexual mode of life,
then prospects of cure are slight. But there are no clearly
marked dividing lines and no certainty in prognosis. A case
considered hopeless may surprise everyone by achieving full
heterosexual adjustment. The subtle interplay of external
and internal influences can never be completely defined and
predicted. Taking into account age, sexual experience, current outlook, and personality factors, the most the psychiatrist can do is to make a rough guess at the probable outcome. But he won't often be proved wrong if he makes a
pessimistic prediction in all cases in which a man has practised homosexuality for years without guilt, and has reached
the late twenties without evincing any sexual interest in
women.

A rough-and-ready sorting out of those unlikely to achieve
a cure is a useful preliminary undertaking. Without going
so far as Dr Stanley-Jones, who regards attempts to change
the sexual orientation in established cases as a moral outrage, one must admit that it is unfair to apply psycho-
analysis, and tear to pieces a person's emotional adjustment,
unless some good will come out of it. Moreover, since psycho-
analysis can only be given to a few, it should be offered to
those most likely to benefit. The ones who stand in greatest
need of treatment are those in the throes of acute neurotic
tension consequent upon a battle with their conscious or unconscious homosexual impulses. The man with the pregnancy phobia was a case in point. As it happened his
impulses were fully conscious, but he would have needed
treatment just as much if the conflict had been so repressed
that it manifested only in panic symptoms. In all cases of
acute anxiety or guilt, secondary to either conscious or unconscious homosexuality, the first stage of treatment is to
bring the patient to a full recognition and acceptance of his
perverse inclinations. Only by first making him come to
terms with his own feelings, and thus allaying his crippling
sense of guilt, can the analyst hope to promote a sufficiently

calm state of mind for the commencement of the second
stage – the exploration of heterosexual inhibitions.

Some might object to this procedure, for the effect of
bringing out repressed tendencies and displaying them for
for what they are might be to convert an anxiety neurotic
into a practising homosexual. A nice question arises as to
which is preferable: neurotic symptoms due to repressed
homosexual desires, or homosexual desires undisguised. Fortunately the risk is not so great as it might seem. An individual with sufficient repugnance of sexual deviation to have
denied and repressed his own true feelings is unlikely to
break out into irresponsible habits when his tendency once
again intrudes upon his conscious thinking.

Apart from prolonged analytic treatment directed towards
conversion to heterosexuality, the psychiatrist can give considerable help in other ways. Many sexual deviants suffer
from neurotic guilt feelings, and to alleviate this source of
distress is a desirable end in itself, and is a task much easier
to accomplish than a conversion to heterosexuality. The
mere fact that the phychiatrist accepts him and enters into
sympathetic relation with him has a beneficial effect on the
guilt-ridden patient. In this way miserable, isolated sufferers,
who hitherto have felt that their shameful peculiarity cuts
them off from all decent human contacts, gain a new faith
in the possibility of helpful relations with other people. Release from neurotic guilt not only relieves their suffering but
makes them more effective members of society. The man
with the pregnancy phobia, once relieved of his abnormal
preoccupation with his shame, would be able to concentrate
on his work and enjoy normal friendships. From a solitary,
drifting, useless character he could be transformed into a
self-respecting individual with normal ambitions and interests, even though his homosexual inclinations might remain. But once again the question arises as to the justifiability of giving free rein to criminal tendencies by removing
the protection of neurotic guilt feelings. The answer lies in
the qualification 'neurotic'. The psychiatrist does not remove
the patient's sense of right and wrong; he can still decide for

himself whether or no to give practical expression to his inclinations. The psychiatrist merely tries to remove the irrational feelings of unworthiness and self-blame that arise from partially repressed conflicts. The neurotic sufferer's sense of guilt comes from internal strife and has no direct relation to the standards of society. He blames himself as much for the existence of homosexual impulses, for which no one would hold him responsible, as for actual lapses, for which he might be sent to prison. Unless relieved of his irrational and undiscriminating sense of guilt, he has no freedom to make a real moral choice. Looked at in this way the psychiatrist's activity no longer appears contrary to accepted standards.

Among those who acquire sufficient equilibrium no longer to experience panic feelings or acute shame on account of their deviant inclinations, many fall a long way short of real contentment. Homosexuals in our society, and especially male homosexuals, cannot be completely reassured because, whether rightly or wrongly, they are in fact the butt of much ill-feeling. They tend to display the reactions typical of any rejected minority. A paranoid attitude, manifest in an uneasy, distrustful approach to people and a hypersensitivity to personal criticism, is all too common among homosexuals. Unfortunately, paranoid attitudes call forth from other people the disapproving, aggressive reactions the sufferer most wants to avoid. Some homosexuals experience great difficulty in their personal relationships on account of their insecurity and touchiness. Even in their love affairs with fellow homosexuals, their sulky, distrustful attitude can mar their relationships and cause much unhappiness and disillusionment. In these problems of personal relations the psychiatrist can give valuable help by means of discussion and superficial analysis.

In addition to the familiar paranoid tendencies, some react in other ways to their feeling of insecurity. A longing for acceptance may cause a person to adopt a rigidly conventional way of life. He does not want to draw attention to himself, and he does want to be one of the herd, so he strives to avoid all taint of unorthodoxy in opinions or behaviour. Few famous homosexuals have been radical reformers. This does not seem a very serious limitation, but it can sometimes produce feelings of severe frustration, as for instance when someone nurses ambitions to branch out into politics, art, social welfare, or other fields but dare not deviate from his normal routine. This type of inhibition occurred in extreme form in the man with the pregnancy phobia. He longed to apply for some worthwhile job but could not do so because he felt he was in too vulnerable a situation to accept a responsible post. The psychiatrist can help with all these difficulties and peculiarities which, fundamentally, arise from feelings of rejection and insecurity. Admittedly homosexuals may have some reason for feeling this way, but often their fears seem exaggerated. Given encouragement they gain confidence in themselves and in their dealings with others, and lose much of their fear-inspired attitudes.

Freud himself believed that for most cases the primary aim of treatment should be to better social adjustment. In a letter to an American mother who sought his advice about her homosexual son he wrote: 'In a certain number of cases we succeed in developing the blighted germs of heterosexual tendencies which are present in every homosexual, in the majority it is no more possible ... What analysis can do for your son runs in a different line. If he is unhappy, neurotic, torn by conflicts, inhibited in his social life, analysis may bring him harmony, peace of mind, full efficiency ...' [68].

Psychological treatment with the limited aim of alleviating distress, improving social capacities, and mending warped attitudes need not involve full psycho-analysis. When conversion to heterosexuality seems improbable, and the aim is merely to promote a better adjustment to homosexuality, deep exploration into childhood sexual fixations is not called for. The desired result can often be achieved by a short series of interviews in which the psychiatrist enters into discussion, and common-sense explanations – so-called superficial psychotherapy. Some cases need a more permanent prop, someone to whom they can turn for advice

and encouragement when they encounter difficulties. For
them the psychiatrist adopts a supportive role. He sees them
from time to time, discusses their immediate difficulties, and
sends them away again with renewed confidence – until the
next time. In recent years the method of group treatment
has been increasingly employed. Patients meet in a group of
about a dozen under the guidance of a psychiatrist and discuss their problems together. Everyone finds it easier to
understand other people's difficulties, and this method has
the advantage of giving patients practical insight into their
troubles and how to cope with them. As accepted members
of a group they feel less isolated and anomalous, and this
is a very important factor in dealing with sexual deviants.
It has a decidedly salutary effect when one of them finds
that the group accepts him as a person in spite of his peculiarity, and that his neurotic defences no longer seem
necessary.

In conclusion, when treating a predominantly homosexual
individual, the first point to consider is whether to aim at
sexual reorientation. Futile attempts at conversion in too
deeply entrenched cases waste time and cause needless
suffering; but cases with a residue of heterosexual feeling,
cases in which the sexual life is immature and consequently
susceptible to different developments, and cases in which
there is great tension and consequently a strong motive for
change, all these have relatively favourable prospects. If
radical change is sought, and sexual inhibition is really deep-
seated, then psycho-analysis is the method of choice – provided, of course, the sufferer has the capacity to cooperate
and to respond. Shorter methods suffice when the aim is
merely to create a better-adjusted homosexual. In these cases
group treatment and superficial psychotherapy are directed
primarily to the relief of guilt and insecurity and to the pro-
motion of happier personal relationships.

The treatment of bisexuals presents a somewhat different
problem. Some persons are emotionally or sexually more inclined to homosexuality, but they force themselves into
heterosexual contacts in order to prove their virility or in

the hope of curing themselves. These can be treated as ordinary homosexuals. But the typical bisexual obtains full satisfaction from the opposite sex, and yet will not relinquish his frequent homosexual indulgence. It is arguable that he suffers from no sexual inhibition, he is a free agent, and therefore psychological treatment is inappropriate. On the other hand, if a married man fails to develop sufficient feeling and responsibility towards his wife and family to prevent his exposing them to the risks attendant upon homosexual escapades, then one suspects a defect of character. The psychological approach to such a case would have to be more in the nature of a character analysis than a frontal attack on sexual habits.

In addition to dealing with requests for remedial treatment, the psychiatrist is often called upon for practical advice. A homosexual may ask bluntly whether it is harmful to strive for complete sexual abstinence. The psychiatrist can, of course, evade the issue by pointing out that the question raises moral and legal issues beyond the medical field; but a more generous way to answer would be to give the pros and cons from the medical standpoint and leave the individual to decide the other issues for himself. It would be fair to say that forced abstinence from fear and guilt often leads to neurotic disorder, but that when strong-minded persons make a deliberate choice to live celibately they sometimes succeed without visible harm. The task becomes less difficult if the individual is fortified by a strong sense of purpose behind his sacrifice, as in the case of a priest, or if he can immerse himself in some cause or activity that will use up the energy he would otherwise expend on the pursuit of love. But for many men, especially those who lack conviction of the value of continence, and those who have been used to sexual experience, the attempt frequently fails, and in any case produces intolerable irritability, restlessness, or depression. In such cases, if the man is determined not to give way, and would rather be castrated than yield, then the psychiatrist can properly help him by giving stilboestrol to reduce the strength of the sexual urge. (See p. 99.) But as a rule homosexuals are unprepared to go to such lengths. Many of them learn that provided their behaviour remains discreet and private, they can indulge without being molested. They are prepared to run the risk of accidental exposure or blackmail. Rarely do homosexuals consider it worthwhile to emigrate to a country where there is no legal discrimination.

The question of marriage presents another thorny problem on which advice may be sought. Some homosexuals elect to marry in spite of their handicap. They gain the benefits of a stable home, as well as protection against social discrimination, but they run the risk of disaster. A man whose inclinations are predominantly homosexual may succeed for a time in the performance of his marital duties (perhaps by conjuring up homosexual thoughts during intercourse) but he is unlikely to make a permanently satisfactory husband either emotionally or physically. Try as he may to remain faithful, the confirmed homosexual tends sooner or later to relapse into his old habits. If he has never confessed his tendency, and his wife discovers it by accident, the emotional shock may lead to the bitterest recriminations, the break-up of the home, and perhaps divorce and public exposure. The psychiatrist has a plain duty to warn an established homosexual against contracting a marriage with a woman who does not know about his problem. Even if she does know, and expresses sympathy, he should make sure she really understands the situation and does not deceive herself that the conversion of a confirmed homosexual is simply a matter of practice. If she thinks her personal charms and her affection will easily wean a man from his perversion, she should be told that there are many homosexuals who can never be won over by feminine influence. Otherwise, finding that her efforts to attract her husband seem merely to irritate and worry him, she might become disillusioned and resentful. Even though it may run counter to strict moral principles, I feel the best advice is to wait until heterosexual intercourse is satisfactorily established before taking on the responsibilities of marriage.

On this, as on other questions concerning homosexuality, the advice must not be too rule-of-thumb. Human nature is so various that the most surprising combinations sometimes succeed. The motive for marriage is important. A great feeling of comradeship, or mutual ambition to rear a family, perhaps forms a better basis than pure social convenience. Some completely homosexual men contract successful partnerships with older women who need an outlet for their motherliness, and are prepared to accept a platonic relationship. Others marry lesbians, and come to a sort of comradely understanding about their sexual adventures. There is also that type of *ménage à trois,* such as was hinted at in the play *The Third Person,* in which there is both a spouse and a homosexual lover. Considering how easy it is for a normal marriage to come to grief through temperamental difficulties, it is understandable that these unorthodox adjustments are peculiarly precarious.

11

Prevention

LEGAL reform, in the sense of removing the penalty for homosexual acts between consenting adults, would help remove a heavy burden of fear and resentment from the minds of a considerable section of the community. As far back as half a century ago Edward Carpenter was campaigning eloquently for greater tolerance [31]. Long before the appointment of a Departmental Committee to consider the advisability of changing the law, the need for reform was pointed out again and again by responsible authorities. Dr E. Glover, the Freudian analyst, has long maintained that the urge to punish sexual deviants betrays a backward outlook [78]. Dr H. Mannheim the criminologist has pointed out that moral indignation is not sufficient grounds for considering homosexual activities anti-social or for punishing them as crimes [135]. Drs Walker and Strauss have expressed the view that imprisonment of the exceptional few who are caught serves no purpose beyond providing pornographic sensation to an ignorant public [191]. In March 1949, the Joint Committee on Psychiatry and the Law appointed by the British Medical Association and the Magistrates' Association published a report which included the following statement: 'The Committee would like to see an early official inquiry into the advisability of the English law being brought into line with continental law in respect of the private conduct of consenting adults' [26].

During the Wolfenden Committee deliberations many official bodies, such as the Royal Medico-Psychological Association and the Church of England Moral Welfare Council, submitted recommendations which were for the most part in favour of this change.

The Wolfenden Report has put the reasons for reform so

cogently, and dealt with the counter-arrangements so carefully, that no useful purpose would be served by reproducing all the points here. Suffice to say that the present law seems both unnecessary and unjust [198]. On any rational standard, heterosexual promiscuity, with its attendant risks of unwanted children and broken homes, does far more damage. It would be fairer if the laws were the same for heterosexuals and homosexuals, and penalties for prostitution, abuse of children, and seduction of minors did not take account of the sex of the participants. Enforced continence can produce unpleasant and sometimes dangerous effects in homosexuals and heterosexuals alike, and many persons will never submit to it whatever the law on the point. If the police were to track down and prosecute all transgressors, there would be utter chaos. The present method of selecting victims for prosecution is so obviously unjust as to bring the processes of law into disrepute. Some persons fear that, given liberty to indulge, homosexual practices would spread so widely as to endanger family life and lower the birth rate. Such fears are grossly exaggerated. No such dramatic result has been observed in Holland or in other countries that already exercise legal tolerance. Pressure of public opinion ensures discretion. Law or no law, exclusive homosexuals are unlikely to make satisfactory parents; and, conversely, persons without heterosexual inhibitions are likely to reproduce regardless of whether or no they indulge occasionally with their own sex. The only worthwhile argument against reform is the religious one, that such acts are against God's will and therefore should not be allowed. But most people would agree that religious beliefs should be a matter for the individual conscience and should not be enforced by legislation.

Apart from the encouragement of blackmail, and the fact that confidential confessions even to doctors are illegal, the present law stirs up some of the very troubles it sets out to combat. Two men cannot share accommodation or associate too closely without suspicion of law-breaking and fear of denunciation. This serves to discourage those who would prefer a settled mode of life, and to encourage casual contacts and promiscuity. Attitudes of despondency and hostility, and reckless behaviour, are fostered by the homosexual's awareness that he is anyhow regarded as a criminal. In the long run, an alteration of the law would probably promote greater circumspection. Furthermore, it would remove from those in authority the temptation to translate personal feeling into dangerous witch hunts.

If private sexual acts between consenting adults ceased to be illegal some 'age of consent' would need to be fixed below which a youth's acquiescence would not be taken as legal justification for sexual relations with an older person. To be consistent the age of consent should be the same for males as for females; certainly few would disagree with a law against sexual relations between a boy under sixteen and an older male. On the other hand, many would feel that a youth of sixteen plus, whose sexual orientation may not yet be fixed and stable, should receive some protection from undue influence by older persons.

The Wolfenden Report, after some discussion about the age of eighteen, finally settles for twenty-one as the age after which private acts might be left to the personal conscience. The Report also makes thirteen other recommendations on points of legal and police practice, none of which seems to have been acted on or even to have attracted much public notice. For instance, they recommend that prosecutions should not be brought when offences are revealed through blackmail. They suggest revising the maximum penalties for the different types of homosexual offence, and reclassifying the crime of buggery so as to place it together with gross indecency in the category of misdemeanours instead of felonies. They suggest that the police should refrain from taking action on offences more than a year old, and that, except in cases of assault, they should not prosecute without first referring to the Director of Public Prosecutions. This would prevent the present arbitrary variations in prosecution policy in different areas.

The desirability of reform appears so obvious that one

must look beyond rational considerations to understand why the question remains a focus of controversy. Dr J. C. Flugel has pointed out that on questions of this sort clashes occur between two opposite points of view, both of which are more closely associated with the emotional development of their protagonists than with the merits of the situation. Persons who in early life have identified strongly with strict parental figures tend to lean towards conservatism and authoritarianism. They are patriotic and loyal to the leader, they uphold traditions and class distinctions, they stress the need for discipline in education and penology, they support religious institutions and the sanctity of family life, and they abhor sexual deviants. The opposite type, those who have undergone an emotional rejection of parental standards, adopt radical opinions, believe in comradeship rather than loyalty to a father figure, dislike the social hierarchy, oppose discipline in education, support penal reform, and are more 'open-minded' about homosexuals [56]. A similar breakdown of social attitudes, with the added refinement of statistical measures, has been carried out by Eysenck, who places individuals on a scale stretching from Toughness and Authoritarianism at one end to Softness and Humanitarianism at the other. At the 'tough' end of the scale are those in favour of such things as flogging for crimes of violence, compulsory sterilization, and corporal punishment for children [52]. It seems that the suggestion of tolerance towards sexual deviants runs counter to a very common constellation of emotionally determined attitudes.

In order to come to a balanced judgement on the matter of the correct attitude to homosexuals, one has to try to cast personal feeling on one side, and to discount the particular prejudices of our society, which has so long unthinkingly stigmatized all such persons as 'perverse', 'heretical', or 'criminal'. The task calls for a high degree of intellectual honesty. Hatred of deviants is so deeply ingrained that, however much an individual may try to preserve a rational approach, he cannot prevent a shudder of disgust at the thought of sexual habits outside his personal experience.

Intellectual realization that our own code is arbitrary, and that some peoples might consider our own kissing habits disgustingly perverse, cannot entirely overcome this revulsion. Neverthless everyone, and especially every doctor, should strive to approach the problem without bias. Though the doctor may not approve the habits of sexual deviants, he can at least try to understand and to give comfort when it is needed.

Important as it may be, both from a practical and a humanitarian point of view, to help an unfortunate minority by introducing legislative changes, the need for tolerance and understanding goes much deeper than this. Homosexuality, as it manifests today, reflects a fault in our social attitudes which no formal statute can hope to cure. Throughout this book a distinction has been drawn between sporadic homosexual behaviour – such as occurs in animals as well as in uninhibited human communities – and the compulsive homosexuality that comes from inhibitions about the opposite sex. In parts of the East, where sexual passion is regarded as no more than a pleasurable pastime, a temporary interruption of the more serious affairs of life, homosexual practices are tolerated as an additional outlet for the predatory male. In this context, homosexual behaviour creates no special problem and the question of abnormality does not arise. The more rigid code of Western culture surrounds heterosexual contacts with a certain aura of anxiety, and at the same time seeks to block the homosexual outlet altogether. As a result, two main deviant types appear. First, the rebel class, those who fail to absorb the common standards and indulge their bisexual impulses in defiance of morality. This is the smaller group, and their sexual problems are often overshadowed by other more specifically anti-social trends. Second, the class of true homosexual, consisting of all those who fall into deviant habits as a result of anxieties and hindrances in the course of heterosexual development. This is much the bigger group, and the one that represents the worse problem in terms of human suffering and social disruption. The measures likely to reduce the numbers of

his group are in the direction of tolerance rather than re-
ression. Paradoxically, a too repressive attitude and a too
arrow view of what is natural and unnatural in the sexual
eld aggravates the situation by instilling at an early age
he fears and anxieties that lead to adult neuroses and
erversions.

An idea of how a changed social outlook might alter the
ituation can be deduced from observations on communi-
ies with a different scale of values. Take, for instance, the
amoan culture as described by Margaret Mead. The
amoans lived serenely and contentedly in a society in which
he accepted standards of good behaviour and social success
vere within easy reach of the average person. Families were
arge, stable, and happy, and child training was easy-going.
When a child behaved badly he was simply carried outside.
Babies were nursed, carried about, and fed generously by
many women besides the mother, and later on the child was
ooked after by his elder sisters, so that exclusive attachments
o parents were hardly possible. Father-son and mother-
daughter rivalries, which provide the raw material for the
Oedipus situation, had no place in their culture. Children
vere as familiar with nude bodies, pregnancy, and copulation
s with the landscape, so no obscene vocabulary was needed
o describe these things. The Samoans found nothing disgusting in sex, and there was no association in thought or
anguage between sex and excretion. Adolescents were
initiated into the arts of love-making by slightly older members of the opposite sex. Thereafter sexual intercourse was
permissible and was undertaken in a light-hearted, un-
hurried spirit, with both parties expecting and achieving full
atisfaction. The adolescent stage presented no special emo-
ional stress, and the onset of menstruation was unaccom-
anied by fear or pain. The very idea of such pain struck
Samoan women as funny when it was explained to them.

Homosexual practices, especially among the young, were
very prevalent, but they were neither frowned upon nor
iven special consideration, being regarded as simply play-
ulness. They had no important or lasting consequences.

Marriage was taken seriously, a partner being chosen by the parents according to social suitability, although the children's wishes were consulted. Thereafter a prolonged liaison followed, and usually resulted in stable marriage, but extra marital sexual adventures could still continue. Great loves, tremendous emotional fixations on one particular person were foreign to Samoan psychology. The important place of marriage and children in the social structure prevented their light-hearted sexual adventures from affecting the even tenor of their lives. Most interestingly, not only was compulsive homosexuality almost unknown (Mead found only one man who shunned sexual intercourse with girls) but frigidity and impotence occurred only as a result of severe physical illness, and sexual neurosis was unheard of. The capacity for intercourse only once a night was counted a sign of senility [141].

In contrast, our own culture, which consists of small, isolated family units, tends to stimulate intense emotional relationships between children and their parents. This charged atmosphere makes for insecurity, and, when coupled with an uneasy, guilt-coloured attitude to awakening sexuality, it provokes the nightmarish 'Freudian' conflicts that lead to neurosis and perversion. An obvious way to tackle the problem is to promote a healthier, less tense approach to sex, and thereby to forestall the development of perversion. A direct attack on individual deviants is not so profitable because there are too many to receive psychiatric attention and many of them are not susceptible to conversion.

To advocate elementary principles of mental hygiene as a cure for the burning problem of homosexuality seems almost impertinent. Every modern manual on child-rearing, every book on popular psychology, explains what to do. But although parents know the answers in theory, they often harbour such inhibitions themselves that they cannot fail to communicate their uneasiness to their offspring. Ideally training in sex should call for no more emotional upheaval than training in any other field. The infant who plays with his genitals should be treated as calmly as one who sucks his

humb. The child who exhibits his own body or explores
ther children's is no more an unnatural horror than one
whose table manners give offence. There is no more reason
o fear he will grow up a sexual maniac than there is to
magine that the boy who helps himself to sweets will be-
ome an armed robber. At every stage of development the
hild benefits from a calm approach to sex. Concealment,
vasion, or lies arouse anxiety and bewilderment. Strained,
eremonial revelation is almost as bad as uneasy suppres-
ion. There is no substitute for the day-to-day, matter-of-
act communication of information by parents who are
hemselves at ease. What is said is often of less importance
han the emotional overtones that go with it. The modern
ystem of imparting theoretical sex instruction in schools
carcely meets the need. The physiology of fertilization is of
ess concern to the adolescent than the question of how far
o go in kissing, petting, and masturbating with the opposite
ex. It is some indication of the inhibitions that still plague
us that so many adolescents would never dream of men-
ioning such intimate matters to their parents, and work out
their own solutions as best they can.

Judging from recent pronouncements in the Courts, and
recent discussions in the Press, there is at present something
of a swing away from the 'free, progressive' outlook back to
old-fashioned morality'. Psychologists have been blamed
for advocating an undisciplined sex life, when in fact they
have only suggested discipline by reason instead of by fear.
The outcry that greets any public revelation of homosexual
practices shows how far current habits of mind still fall short
of theoretical enlightment. People are shocked by and react
sharply to what they read about homosexuality in the Sunday papers, but the Courts continually deal with all kinds
of sexual matters – incest, bestiality, and so forth – which
are far more shocking than anything printed in newspapers.

One argument against a liberal attitude to sex is the
theory that freedom leads to social decadence. Psycho-
analysts have taught that provided the individual does not
succumb to neurosis, enforced sexual continence can have

the effect of re-directing into socially useful channels th
energies that would otherwise be dissipated in the satisfa
tion of sex urges. The thesis has been put most learnedly b
Unwin, who made a study of the marital regulations
eighty uncivilized societies. He concluded that developmen
of social organization, beginnings of discovery, expansic
into neighbouring territory, in fact all the signs of an ene
getic society, made their appearance only when sexual free
dom was curtailed. Societies in which pre-nuptial and extr
marital intercourse were allowed remained on a dead lev
of animal sloth [190]. This point of view can be taken to
far. Unwin himself pointed out that strictly monogamo
societies, in which there was no sexual outlet except throug
the legitimate spouse, did not usually survive for long. B
tween racial suicide by complete denial of sex and soci
anarchy through selfish unrestraint there must be som
reasonable compromise. The important point is that wha
ever compromise we choose for ourselves or teach to ou
children should be based on informed opinion, free from
the taboos of the savage, and tolerant towards othe
standards.

It must be admitted that no amount of mental hygien
is likely to eradicate homosexuality entirely. However on
tries to smooth the path of normal development, so tha
more and more can attain full stature, a few will always ru
into difficulties and find solace in this half-way adjustmen
Neurosis and perversions have always been with us, and,
Dr Glover points out, 'We cannot say whether even a sati
factory spread of psychological knowledge, upbringing, an
treatment would bring about a decisive modification
ancient patterns of sexual habit and regulation.' [79]. It
clear that the use of harsh measures in an attempt to bloc
the homosexual outlet altogether would not succeed, an
might well make matters worse by re-introducing that atmo
phere of fear that is the root cause of the trouble. Perhaj
the most civilized attitude towards sexual deviants would b
similar to the present attitude to unmarried persons. Whil
recognizing that they are missing a rewarding experienc

nd are not contributing directly to the task of child-rearing, ve realize that they may be temperamentally unsuited to narried life, and that they may serve the community use- ully in other ways besides bringing up a family of their wn. No one would suggest passing laws to force them into narriage, for the results would obviously be disastrous. But oleration of sexual deviants is not the same as encourage- nent. No doctor should advise a young person to rest con- ent with a homosexual orientation without first giving a rave warning about the frustration and tragedy inherent n this mode of life.

LIST OF REFERENCES
AND INDEX

LIST OF REFERENCES

[1] Allen, Clifford. *The Sexual Perversions and Abnormalitie*
London, 1949.

[2] Allen, Clifford. *The Adrenal Cortex and Intersexualit*
London, 1938.

[3] Allen, Clifford. *Homosexuality. Its Nature, Causation an*
Treatment. London, 1958.

[4] Andenaes, J. 'Recent trends in the Criminal Law an
Penal System in Norway'. *Brit. Journ. Delinquenc*
1954, 5, pp. 21–9.

[5] 'Anomaly'. *The Invert.* London, 1927.

[6] Anon. *Plain Reasons for the Growth of Sodomy in Eng*
land. London, *circa* 1730.

[7] Apfelberg, B., *et al.* 'A Psychiatric Study of 250 Sex Offend
ers'. *American Journ. Psychiatry* 1944, 100, pp. 762–

[8] Appel, K. E. 'Endocrine Studies in Cases of Homosexu
ality'. *Archiv. Neurology and Psychiatry* 1937, 3'
pp. 1206–7.

[9] Bailey, D. Sherwin. *Homosexuality and the Western Chris*
tian Tradition. London, 1955.

[10] Barahal, H. S. 'Constitutional Factors in Male Homo
sexuals'. *Psychiatric Quarterly* 1939, 13, pp. 391–40C

[11] Barahal, H. S. 'Testosterone in Psychotic Male Homo
sexuals'. *Psychiatric Quarterly* 1940, 14, pp. 319–29

[12] Bauer, J. 'Homosexuality as an Endocrinological, Psycho
logical and Genetic Problem'. *Journ. Criminal Psy*
chopathology 1940, 2, pp. 188–97.

[13] Beach, F. A. 'Experimental Studies of Sexual Behaviour i
Male Animals'. *Journ. Clinical Endocrinology* 1944
4, pp. 126–34.

[14] Beach, F. A. 'Sexual Behaviour in Animals and Men
The Harvey Lectures, 1947–8. Springfield, Illinois
1950.

[15] Bender, L., and Grugett, A. 'A follow-up report on childre
who had a typical sexual experience'. *Am. Journ*
Orthopsychiatry 1952, 22, pp. 825–37.

[16] Bender, L., and Paster, S. 'Homosexual Trends in Child
ren'. *American Journ. Orthopsychiatry* 1941, 11, pp
730–44.

[17] Benedict, R. *Patterns of Culture.* Boston, 1934.

[18] Benedict, R. 'Sex in Primitive Society'. *American Journ. Orthopsychiatry* 1939, 9, pp. 570–4.

[19] Bergler, E. 'The Myth of a New National Disease; Homosexuality and the Kinsey Report'. *Psychiatry Quarterly* 1948, 22, pp. 66–88.

[20] Bergler, E. *Neurotic Counterfeit Sex*. New York, 1951.

[21] Bergmann, M. S. 'Homosexuality in the Rorschach Test'. *Bulletin Menninger Clinic* 1945, 9, pp. 78–83.

[22] Berkman, A. *Prison Memoirs of an Anarchist*. London, 1926.

[23] Berthe, E. 'Die dorische Knabenliebe'. *Rhein. Mus.* 1907, 62 (n.F.), pp. 438–75.

[24] Bosselman, B., and Skorodin, B. 'Masculinity and Femininity in Psychotic Patients'. *American Journ. Psychiatry* 1941, 97, pp. 699–702.

[25] Brill, A. A. 'Homo-eroticism and Paranoia'. *American Journ. Psychiatry* 1934, 13, pp. 957–74.

[26] British Medical Ass. and Magistrates' Ass. 'Criminal Law and Sexual Offenders'. *Brit. Medical Journ.* (Supplement) 12 March 1949, pp. 135–40.

[27] Brown, D. G. 'Inversion and Homosexuality'. *Am. Journ. Orthopsychiatry* 1958, 28, pp. 424–9.

[28] Burton, R. *Arabian Nights*. Benares (Kamashastra Soc.), 1885. Terminal Essay. Vol X. pp. 205–54.

[29] Calder, W. 'The Sexual Offender'. *Brit. Journ. Delinquency* 1955, 6, pp. 26–40.

[30] Caprio, F. S. *Female Homosexuality*. New York, 1954.

[31] Carpenter, E. *The Intermediate Sex*. London, 1907.

[32] Cason, H. 'A Case of Sexual Psychopathy'. *Journ. Clin. Psychopathology* 1947, 8, pp. 785–800.

[33] Chapman, A. H., and Reese, D. G. 'Homosexual Signs in Rorschachs of Early Schizophrenics'. *Journ. Clin. Psychology* 1953, 9, pp. 30–2.

[34] Comfort, Alex. *Sexual Behaviour in Society*. London, 1950.

[35] Cory, D. W. (pseud.) *The Homosexual in America*. New York, 1951.

[36] Cory, D. W. 'Homosexuality in Prison'. *Journ. Social Therapy*, 1955, 1, pp. 137–40.

[37] Curran, D. (I) 'Sexual Perversions and their Treatment'. *The Practitioner* 1947, 158, pp. 343–8.

[38] Curran, D. (II) *Psychological Medicine*. Edinburgh, 1943.

[39] Curran, D., and Parr, D. 'Homosexuality: An analysis of 100 male cases'. *Brit. Medical Journ.* 1957, I, pp. 797–801.

[40] Darke, R. 'Heredity as an Etiological Factor in Homosexuality'. *Journ. Nervous and Mental Dis.* 1948, 107, pp. 251–68.

[41] Davis, K. B. *Factors in the Sex Life of 2,200 Women.* New York, 1929.

[42] Deutsch, A. 'Vice Squad'. *Collier's,* 28 May 1954.

[43] Deutsch, H. *The Psychology of Woman.* London, 1946.

[44] Devereux, G. 'Institutionalised Homosexuality of the Mohave Indians'. *Human Biology* 1937, 9, pp. 498–527.

[45] Dickinson, G. L. *The Greek View of Life.* London, 1896.

[46] Doshay, L. J. *The Boy Sex Offender and his Later Career.* New York, 1943.

[47] Dunn, C. W. 'Stilboestrol-induced Gynecomastia in the Male'. *Journ. American Medical Ass.* 1940, 115, pp. 2263–4.

[48] East, W. Norwood, *et al.* 'The Sociological Aspects of Homosexuality'. *Medico Legal Journ.* 1947, 15, pp. 11–23.

[49] Ellis, A. 'The Sexual Psychology of Human Hermaphrodites'. *Psychosomatic Medicine* 1945, 7, pp. 108–25.

[50] Ellis, A. 'The effectiveness of psychotherapy with individuals who have severe homosexual problems'. *Journ. Consulting Psychology* 1956, 20, pp. 191–5.

[51] Ellis, H. *Studies in the Psychology of Sex.* Vol. II, New York, 1936.

[52] Eysenck, H. J. *The Psychology of Politics.* London, 1954.

[53] Fenichel, O. *The Psychoanalytic Theory of Neurosis.* New York, 1945.

[54] Finger, F. W. 'Sex Beliefs and Practices among Male College Students'. *Journ. Abnormal and Social Psychology* 1947, 42, pp. 57–67.

[55] Fishman, J. F. *Sex in Prison.* London, 1935.

[56] Flugel, J. C. *Man, Morals and Society,* London, 1945.

[57] Foote, R. M. 'Diethylstilboestrol in the Management of Psychopathological States'. *Journ. Nervous and Mental Dis.* 1944, 99, pp. 928–35.

[58] Ford, C. S., and Beach, F. A. *Patterns of Sexual Behaviour.* London, 1952.

[59] Foss, G. L. 'The Influence of Urinary Androgens on Sexuality in Women'. *Lancet* 1951, pp. 667–9.

[60] Fox, L. W. *The English Prison and Borstal Systems.* London, 1952.

[61] Freeman, T. 'Clinical and theoretical observations on male homosexuality'. *Internat. Journ. Psycho-analysis* 1955, 36, pp. 335–47.

[62] Freud, S. *Three Essays on the Theory of Sexuality* (trans. J. Strachey) London, 1949.

[63] Freud, S. 'On Narcissism: An Introduction'. *Collected Papers*, vol. 4, pp. 30–50.

[64] Freud, S. 'On the Transformation of Instincts, with special reference to Anal Erotism'. (1916) *Collected Papers*, vol. 2, pp. 164–71.

[65] Freud, S. 'Character and Anal Erotism'. (1908) *Collected Papers*, vol. 2, pp. 45–50.

[66] Freud, S. 'A Case of Paranoia'. (1911) *Collected Papers*, vol. 3, pp. 387–470.

[67] Freud, S. 'The Psychogenesis of a Case of Homosexuality in a Woman'. (1920) *Collected Papers*, vol. 2, pp. 202–31.

[68] Freud, S. 'Letter to an American Mother'. *American Journ. Psychiatry* 1951, 108, p. 252.

[69] Freund, J., *et al.* 'On the validity and reliability of phalloplethysmographic Diagnosis of some sexual deviations'. *Review of Czechoslovak Medicine* 1958, 4, pp. 145–51.

[70] Gaaremstroom, J. H. 'Sexual Development of Fowls derived from Eggs Treated with Oestradiol Benzoate'. *Journ. Endocrinology* 1940, pp. 247–54.

[71] Garland, Rodney. *The Heart in Exile.* London, 1953.

[72] Geddes, D. P. (Ed.) *An Analysis of the Kinsey Reports on Sexual Behaviour.* New York, 1954.

[73] Gibbens, T. C. N. 'The sexual behaviour of young criminals'. *Journ. Mental Science* 1957, 103, pp. 527–40.

[74] Gide, André. *Journal 1889–1939.* Paris, 1939.

[75] Giese, H. *L'Homosexualité de l'homme.* Paris (Payot), 1959.

[76] Glass, S. J., *et al.* 'Sex Hormone Studies in Male Homosexuality'. *Journ. Clin. Endocrinology* 1940, 26, pp. 590–4.

[77] Glass, S. J., and Johnson, R. H. 'Limitations and Complica
tions of Organotherapy in Male Homosexuality
Journ. Clin. Endocrinology 1940, 4, pp. 540–4.

[78] Glover, E. 'The Social and Legal Aspects of Sexual Ab
normality'. Medico Legal Journ. 1945, 13, pp. 133–48

[79] Glover, Edward. 'Victorian Ideas of Sex'. Ideas and Belief
of the Victorians. London, 1949.

[80] Golla, F. L., and Hodge, R. S. 'Hormone Treatment of th
Sexual Offender'. Lancet 1949, i, p. 1006.

[81] Greco, M. C., and Wright, J. C. 'The Correctional Institu
tion in the Etiology of Chronic Homosexuality
American Journ. Orthopsychiatry 1944, 14, pp. 295
307.

[82] Greenblatt, R. B. 'Hormonal Factors in Libido'. Journ
Clin. Endocrinology 1943, 3, pp. 305–6.

[83] Greenspan, H., and Campbell, J. D. 'The Homosexual as
Personality Type'. American Journ. Psychiatry 1945
101, pp. 682–9.

[84] Group for the Advancement of Psychiatry. Rep. 1955, No
30. 'On homosexuality, with particular emphasis on
this problem in governmental agencies.'

[85] Grygier, T. G. 'Psychometric aspects of homosexuality'
Journ. Mental Science 1957, 103, pp. 514–26.

[86] Hackfield, A. W. 'Über die Kastration bei vierzig sexuel
Abnormen'. Monatschrift für Psychiatrie und Neur
ologie 1933, 87, p. 1.

[87] Hamilton, D. M. 'Some Aspects of Homosexuality in rela
tion to Total Personality Development'. Psychiatri
Quarterly 1939, 13, pp. 229–44.

[88] Hamilton, G. V. A Research in Marriage. New York, 1929

[89] Hamilton, J. B. 'Treatment of Sexual Under-developmen
with Synthetic Male Hormone Substance'. Journ
Clin. Endocrinology 1937, 21, p. 649.

[90] Harrison, T. Savage Civilisation. London, 1937.

[91] Hastings, D. W. 'A Paranoid Reaction with Manifes
Homosexuality'. Archiv. Neurology and Psychiatry
1941, 45, pp. 379–81.

[92] Hemphill, R. E., et al. 'A factual study of male homosexu
ality'. Brit. Medical Journ. June 1958, pp. 1317–23.

[93] Henry, G. W. Sex Variants. London and New York, 1948

[94] Henry, G. W. All the Sexes. New York, 1955.

[95] Henry, G. W., and Galbraith, H. M. 'Constitutional Factors in Homosexuality'. *American Journ. Psychiatry* 1934, 13, pp. 1249–67.

[96] Henry, J. *Who Lie in Gaol*. London, 1952.

[97] Hirschfeld, M. *Die Homosexualität des Mannes und des Weibes*. Berlin, 1920.

[98] Hirschfeld, M. *Sexual Anomalies and Perversions*. London, 1944.

[99] Holloway. *The Phoenix of Sodom*. London, 1813.

[100] Hooker, E. 'The adjustment of the male overt homosexual'. *Journ. Projective Techniques* 1957, 21, pp. 18–31.

[101] Hooker, E. 'Preliminary analysis of group behaviour of homosexuals. *Journ. of Psychology* 1956, 42, pp. 217–25.

[102] Hyde, H. M. *The Trials of Oscar Wilde*. London, 1948.

[103] James, R. E. 'Precipitating Factors in Acute Homosexual Panic (Kempf's Disease) with a Case Presentation'. *Quarterly Rev. Psychiatry and Neurology* 1947, 2, pp. 530–3.

[104] Jenkins, M. 'The effect of segregation on the sex behaviour of the white rat'. *Genetic Psychol. Monographs* 1928, 3, pp. 461–71.

[105] Jonas, C. H. 'An objective approach to the personality and environment in homosexuality'. *Psychiatric Quarterly* 1944, 18, pp. 626–41.

[106] Jowitt, F. W. 'Medicine and the Law' (The Twenty-Eighth Maudsley Lecture). *Journal of Mental Science*, 1954, 100, pp. 351–9.

[107] Kallman, F. J. 'Twin Sibships and the Study of Male Homosexuality'. *American Journ. Human Genetics* 1952, 4, pp. 136–46.

[108] Kallman, F. J. 'Comparative Twin Study of the Genetic Aspects of Male Homosexuality'. *Journ. Nervous and Mental Dis.* 1952, 115, pp. 283–98.

[109] Karpman, B. 'Sex Life in Prison'. *Journ. Crim. Law and Criminology* 1948, 38, pp. 475–86.

[110] Kempe, G. T. 'The Homosexual in Society'. *Brit. Journ. Delinquency* 1954, 5, pp. 4–20.

[111] Kinsey, A. C. 'Criteria for a Hormonal Explanation of Homosexuality'. *Journ. Clin. Endocrinology* 1941, 1, pp. 424–8.

[112] Kinsey, A. C. *et al. Sexual Behaviour in the Human Male.* (Saunders) London and Philadelphia, 1948.

[113] Kinsey, A. C. *et al. Sexual Behaviour in the Human Female.* London and Philadelphia, 1953.

[114] Klein, H. R. and Horwitz, W. A. 'Psychosexual Factors in the Paranoid Phenomena'. *American Journ. Psychiatry* 1949, 105, pp. 697–701.

[115] Kubie, L. S. 'Psychiatric Implications of the Kinsey Report'. *Psychosomatic Medicine* 1948, 10, pp. 95–106.

[116] Lagache, D. 'Homosexuality and Jealousy'. *Internat. Journ. Psycho-Analysis* 1950, 31, pp. 24–31.

[117] Lambert, K. 'Homosexuals'. *Medical Press* 1954, 232, pp. 523–6.

[118] Landis, C. *Sex in Development.* New York and London, 1940.

[119] Landtman, G. *The Kiwai Papuans of British New Guinea.* London, 1927.

[120] Lang, T. 'Studies in the Genetic Determination of Homosexuality'. *Journ. Nervous and Mental Dis.* 1940, 92, pp. 55–64.

[121] Lange, J. *Crime as Destiny: a Study of Criminal Twins* (trans.). London, 1930.

[122] Lewinsky, H. 'Features from a Case of Homosexuality'. *Psychoanalytic Quarterly* 1952, 21, pp. 344–54.

[123] Lewis, C. S. *Surprised by Joy,* London, 1955.

[124] Licht, H. *Sexual Life in Ancient Greece* (trans.). London, 1931.

[125] Liddicoat, R. 'Homosexuality: Results of a survey'. Thesis. Univ. of Witwatersrand, 1956. (See *Brit. Med. Journ.,* 9 Nov. 1957).

[126] Loeser, L. H. 'The sexual psychopath in military service'. *Amer. Journ. Psychiatry* 1945, 102, pp. 92–101.

[127] London, L. S. and Caprio, F. S. *Sexual Deviations.* Washington, 1950.

[128] Lorand, S. *Clinical Studies in Psychoanalysis.* New York, 1950.

[129] Lurie, L. A. 'The Endocrine Factor in Homosexuality'. *American Journ. Medical Science* 1944, 208, pp. 176–84.

[130] MacKinnon, J. 'The Homosexual Woman'. *American Journ. Psychiatry* 1947, 103, pp. 661–4.

[131] Mackwood, J. C. 'Remedial and Educational Psychotherapy during Penal Detention' in *The Roots of Crime*. Ed. Norwood East, London, 1954.

[132] Mackwood, J. C. 'A Note on the Psychotherapeutic Treatment of Homosexuality in Prison'. *Medical Practitioner* 1947, 217, pp. 217–19.

[133] Malinowski, B. *The Sexual Life of Savages in North-West ern Melanesia*. London, 1929.

[134] Mannheim, H. *Criminal Justice and Social Reconstruction*. London, 1946.

[135] Mannheim, H. 'Some Criminological Aspects of Homosexuality'. *Medical Practitioner* 1947, 217, pp. 210–12.

[136] Masters, W. H., and Magallon, D. T. 'Androgen Administration in the Post Menopausal Woman'. *Journ. Clin. Endocrinology* 1950, 10, p. 348.

[137] Maurois, André. *The Quest for Proust*. London, 1950.

[138] Mead, M. *Sex and Temperament*. London, 1935.

[139] Mead, M. *Male and Female*. New York, 1949.

[140] Mead, M. *Growing Up in New Guinea*. London, 1931.

[141] Mead, M. *Coming of Age in Samoa*. New York, 1928.

[142] Meier, M. H. E. *Histoire de l'amour grec* (trans. L. R. de Pogey-Castries). Paris, 1952.

[143] Money, J., *et al.* 'Imprinting and the establishment of gender role'. *Archiv. Neurology and Psychiatry* 1957, 77, pp. 333–6.

[144] Moore, T. V. 'The Pathogenesis and Treatment of Homosexual Disorders'. *Journ. Personality* 1945, 14, pp. 47–83.

[145] Myerson, A., and Neustadt, R. 'Androgen Excretion in Urine in various Neuropsychiatric Conditions'. *Archiv. Neurology and Psychiatry* 1940, 44, p. 689.

[146] Myerson, A., and Neustadt, R. 'Essential Male Homosexuality and Results of Treatment'. *Archiv. Neurology and Psychiatry* 1946, 55, pp. 291–3.

[147] Nathan, P. *The Psychology of Fascism*. London, 1943.

[148] Nelson, V. *Prison Days and Nights*. Boston, 1930.

[149] Neodoma, K. 'Homosexuality in Sexological Practice'. *Internat. Journ. Sexology* 1951, 4, pp. 219–24.

[150] Norman, J. P. 'Evidence and Clinical Significance of Homosexuality in 100 Unanalysed Cases of Demen-

tia Praecox'. *Journ. Nervous and Mental Dis.* 1948, 107, pp. 484–9.

[151] O'Connor, W. A. 'Some notes on suicide'. *Brit. Journ. Medical Psychol.* 1948, 21, pp. 222–8.

[152] Oraison, M. *Vie chrétienne et problèmes de la sexualité.* Paris, 1952. (Withdrawn.)

[153] Owensby, N. M. 'Homosexuality and Lesbianism Treated with Metrazol'. *Journ. Nervous and Mental Dis.* 1940, 92, pp. 65–6.

[154] Pare, C. M. B. 'Homosexuality and chromosomal sex'. *Journ. Psychosomatic Res.* 1956, 1, pp. 247–51.

[155] Perloff, W. H. 'The Role of Hormones in Human Sexuality'. *Psychosomatic Medicine* 1949, 11, pp. 133–9.

[156] Ploscowe, M. *Sex and the Law.* New York, 1951.

[157] Poe, J. S. 'The Successful Treatment of a 40-Year-Old Passive Homosexual'. *Psychoanalytic Review* 1952, 29, pp. 23–33.

[158] Radzinowicz, L. *Sexual Offences.* London, 1957.

[159] Rado, S. 'A Critical Examination of the Concept of Bisexuality'. *Psychosomatic Medicine* 1940, 20, 2, pp. 459–67.

[160] Ramsey, G. V. 'The Sexual Development of Boys'. *American Journ. Psychology* 1943, 56, pp. 217–33.

[161] Rasmussen, A. 'Die Bedeutung Sexueller Attentate auf Kinder unter 14 Jahren für die Entwicklung von Geisteskrankheiten und Characteranomalien'. *Acta Psychiatrica et Neurologica* 1934, 9, pp. 351–433.

[162] Rasmussen, E. W. 'Experimental homosexual behaviour in male albino rats'. *Acta Psychologica* 1955, 11, pp. 303–34.

[163] Regardie, F. I. 'Analysis of a Homosexual'. *Psychiatric Quarterly* 1949, 23, pp. 548–66.

[164] Rosanoff, A. J. *Manual of Psychiatry and Mental Hygiene.* New York, 1938.

[165] Rosanoff, W. R., and Murphy, F. E. 'The Basal Metabolic Rate ... etc. in Homosexuals'. *American Journ. Psychiatry* 1944, 101, pp. 97–9.

[166] Rosenfeld, H. 'Remarks on the Relationship of Male Homosexuality to Paranoia ...' *Internat. Journ. Psycho-analysis* 1949, 30, pp. 36–47.

[167] Ruskin, S. H. 'Analysis of Sex Offenders among Male Psy-

chiatric Patients'. *American Journ. Psychiatry* 1941, 97, pp. 955–68.

[168] Schneck, J. M. 'Some Aspects of Homosexuality in Relation to Hypnosis'. *Psychoanalytic Review* 1950, 37, pp. 351–7.

[169] Schrenck-Notzing, A. von. *Therapeutic Suggestion in Psychopathia Sexualis with especial reference to Contrary Sexual Instinct* (trans. C. G. Chaddock). London, 1895.

[170] Schwarz, H. 'A Case of Character Disorder'. *Bull. Menninger Clinic* 1952, 16, pp. 20–30.

[171] Sevringhaus, E. L., and Chornyak, J. 'A Study of Homosexual Adult Males'. (17-keto-steroid assays). *Psychosomatic Medicine* 1945, 7, pp. 302–5.

[172] Sherwin, R. V. *Sex and the Statutory Law.* New York, 1949.

[173] Slater, E., and Slater, P. 'A Study in the Assessment of Homosexual Traits'. *Brit. Journ. Medical Psychology* 1947, 21, pp. 61–74.

[174] Smalldon, J. L. 'The Etiology of Chronic Alcoholism'. *Psychiatric Quarterly* 1933, 4, pp. 640–61.

[175] Smith, A. Heckstall. *Eighteen Months.* London, 1954.

[176] Smith, C. E. 'The homosexual federal offender'. *Journ. Criminal Law and Criminology* 1954, 44, pp. 582–91.

[177] Soddy, K. 'Homosexuality'. *Lancet* 1954, 267, pp. 541–6.

[178] Stanley-Jones, D. 'Royal Society of Medicine Symposium on Homosexuality'. *Medical Press* Sept. 1947, p. 213.

[179] Stanley-Jones, D. 'Sexual Inversion: an Ethical Study'. *Lancet,* 1947, i, pp. 366–9.

[180] Stekel, W. 'Is Homosexuality Curable?' *Psychoanalytic Review* 1930, 17, pp. 443–5.

[181] Swyer, G. I. M. 'Homosexuality: The Endocrinological Aspects'. *The Practitioner* 1954, 172, pp. 374–7.

[182] Symonds, J. A. *A Problem in Greek Ethics.* London, 1901.

[183] Taylor, F. J. 'Homosexual Offences and their Relation to Psychotherapy'. *Brit. Medical Journ.* 4 October 1947, pp. 525–9.

[184] Taylor, G. R. *Sex in History.* London, 1953.

[185] Terman, L. M., and Miles, C. C. *Sex and Personality.* New York, 1936.

[186] Thompson, C. 'Changing Concepts of Homosexuality in Psycho-analysis'. *Psychiatry* 1947, 10, pp. 183–9.

[187] Thompson, G. N. 'Electro-shock and other Therapeut Considerations in Sexual Psychopathy'. *Journ. Ner vous and Mental Dis.* 1949, 109, pp. 531–9.

[188] Thornton, N. (I) 'Some Mechanisms of Paranoia'. *Psych analytic Review* 1948, 35, pp. 290–4.

[189] Thornton, N. (II) 'The Relation Between Crime and Ps chopathic Personality'. *Journ. Criminal Law a Criminology* 1951, 42, pp. 199–204.

[190] Unwin, J. C. *Sex and Culture.* Oxford, 1934.

[191] Walker, K. and Strauss, E. B. *Sexual Disorders in the Ma* London, 1942.

[192] West, D. J. 'Parental Relationships in male homosexualit *Internat. Journ. Social Psychiatry* 1959, 5, pp. 85–9

[193] Westwood, G. *Society and the Homosexual.* London, 195

[194] Wildeblood, P. *Against the Law.* London, 1955.

[195] Wildeblood, P. *A Way of Life,* London, 1956.

[196] Winner, A. L. 'Homosexuality in Women'. *Medical Pract tioner* 1947, 217, pp. 219–20.

[197] Witschi, E., and Mengert, W. F. 'Endocrine Studies o Human Hermaphrodites and their Bearing upon th Interpretation of Homosexuality'. *Journ. Clin. End crinology* 1942, 2, pp. 279–86.

[198] Wolfenden: *Report of the Committee on Homosexual O fences and Prostitution* Cmnd. 247. London, 1958.

[199] Wortis, J. 'A Note on the Body-build of the Male Hom sexual'. *American Journ. Psychiatry* 1937, 93, p 1121–5.

[200] Wortis, J. 'Intersexuality and Effeminacy in a Male Hom sexual'. *American Journ. Orthopsychiatry* 1940, 1 pp. 567–9.

[201] Wright, C. A. 'Endocrine Aspects of Homosexuality *Medical Rec.* New York 1935, 142, p. 407.

[202] Zamansky, H. S. 'An investigation of the psychoanalyt theory of delusions'. *Journ. Personality* 1958, 26, p 410–25.

[203] Zuckerman, S. *The Social Life of Monkeys and Apes.* Lo don, 1932.

INDEX